Adult Children Of Narcissistic Parents

A Guide to Understanding Narcissism and Overcoming
Relationships With Mothers and Fathers With
Narcissistic Personality Disorder

By

Lorna Mayers

© **Copyright 2019 by Lorna Mayers**

All rights reserved.

The information herein is offered for informational purposes solely, and is universal as so. The presentation of the information is without contract or any type of guarantee assurance.

The trademarks that are used are without any consent, and the publication of the trademark is without permission or backing by the trademark owner. All trademarks and brands within this book are for clarifying purposes only and are owned by the owners themselves, not affiliated with this document.

Contents

Introduction

E very plant is the result of a seed that was sown. It has been proven, and is now common knowledge, that, as far as the human being is regarded, are a product of the combination of the various pieces of the education received in childhood and all the values we are taught from all the environments we have interacted with as we grew into adults.

Every adult at some point developed their value system and life's paradigm based on the experiences they had in childhood, the things they learned in the course of their journey to adulthood, and everything they were taught by their parents or guardians. The adult we become, and the values we have are an indication of the family by which we were raised. Our past and present choices are a direct reflection of our upbringing.

Many have come to realize that every human attitude is unique, while some behaviors are similar. The similarity in characters has helped psychological researchers to define a person or predict the subsequent character of a person and the reason behind their actions. Some characters have been termed as a disorder because they are not predictable or similar to people of the same culture, level of education, age or even gender.

Personality disorders are characters exhibited by a person that is having an unhealthy mental way of thinking, acting or behaving around other people. These behaviors are mostly not acceptable in society. A personality disorders can be divided into three main groups.

The first group of people with personality disorders are usually people who have some kind of odd and eccentric behavior or method of thinking. People who fall into this group are usually paranoid, have little or no social relationships and have a line of thought about what they believe in. The second group of people with personality disorder are usually very emotional, dramatic and they may be unpredictable in their behavior and how they think, while the third group of people with personality disorder exhibit a lot of fear, and they are overly anxious. This disorder can make them be avoidant, dependent, obsessive or compulsive.

While the first and last group of people with a personality disorder may be predictable, the second group of personality disorder is not always as predictable. Narcissistic personality disorder falls in the second group of personality disorders.

The term "Narcissism" simply refers to those with a magnified sense of self-worth. Someone who displays a narcissistic disposition probably shows the trait of the disorder referred to as Narcissistic Personality Disorder (NPD).

A personality and psychological disorder such as narcissism can influence the entire behavior and character of a person. Any kind of personality disorder will affect a person's character. This is because it influences the way an individual will think, act and relate to other people. According to the American Psychiatric Association, "The essential features of a personality disorder are the impairments on the personality's (self and interpersonal) functioning and the presence of pathological personality traits."

The term "Narcissism" derives from the term Narcissus – the name of a Greek mythological figure – which was the son of a god. The story narrates how Narcissus fell in love with his reflection by the waters of a spring. He imagined himself to be very handsome and the strongest god. He, therefore, desired that everyone paid homage to him and admired his beauty and strength. Narcissus thought of several means to gain admiration from people without making them see his desire for admiration. The only option available to Narcissus to convince people to admire him was to make them feel loved, shower praises on them, and even offer help before it was asked. It was said that the birds sang praises about his loving nature and even the maidens worshipped his beauty and kindness.

However, the story of Narcissus was short-lived because he stopped being kind to people, and hence the praises were halted. Thus, he became angry with the outcome of events because he wanted more admiration from people and there was no one willing to do so.

The story of Narcissus has changed over time, but this is the core foundation of the characters exhibited by many narcissists today. The attributes of people living with the narcissist disorder and their obsession with themself have become a major topic all over the world. Many have researched on this unique and strange personality disorder with the hope of finding a permanent solution.

As people close to the narcissist may be influenced to behave like the narcissist, it has also been noted that children born to a narcissist may end up being like their parents if urgent intervention is not done to save the situation. A narcissist obsession to reflect and extend themselves in other people around them is achieved through control, domination, guilt-tripping, and possession via an act of love that is tainted with selfishness.

Research has shown that most of us, almost everyone on earth, are prone to exhibiting narcissism. Everyone, at some point, possibly unconsciously, will exhibit narcissistic tendencies once in a while. These tendencies only become problematic when they affect a person's ability to interact with others. This occurs when a personality disorder of any kind becomes the reason for a dysfunctional relationship of any kind.

Individuals with narcissistic personality disorder exhibit outrageous certainty, long for consideration, and show little empathy for other individuals. Be that as it may, beneath this exteriority of certainty, they experience the ill effects of this powerless confidence. They require a steady flow of approval in all their relationships, accompanied by sentiments of pity or deficiency and powerlessness in sealing their enduring connections.

Usually, narcissists behave the way they do because they are not satisfied with who they are or what they are currently doing. This emptiness is filled when a narcissist meets someone or something to supply what is craved for. The narcissist supply is a person or a thing from which or whom the narcissist draws out what he needs. The supply normally doesn't know they are merely filling up as a need of this person. This supply may feel that constant admiration, show of love, kindness and great care is a normal way of life for people who live in a civilized society. However, with careful consideration, the supply may understand that more energy, love, power, strength, and care is being drained from him or her than what the narcissist is willing to offer in return. A narcissist is someone who lacks self-satisfaction and fulfillment. They are never good enough for themselves. They cling to others for their sense of self-worth. Relying on others for satisfaction and fulfillment. They do not exactly accept themselves for who they are. This is reflected in the way in which they relate with others, particularly when kids are involved.

In most cases, a narcissist supply or a narcissist victim begins their stories about how charming, loving, and caring the narcissist has been. Gradually, the story changes like an unstable but beautiful rollcoaster until the moment in which the narcissist will become very abusive. Narcissists are known for their charisma and good ability to make a person love who they are almost immediately. This feeling is normally referred to as the love bomb game. It catches the unsuspecting victim, and there will be no traces to show that the narcissist has other negative intentions. This game quickly leads to a fast-emotional relationship that may make the victim bear a child for the narcissist.

A narcissist parent cannot love unconditionally nor give unlimited affection. This affects the children involved; they lack a sense of security or being cared for. The children of narcissist parents are constantly starved and deprived of parental love. They are pushed into a consistent state of need and longing for love and an affirmation that they belong in the family. This longing for affection and also acknowledgment eventually becomes a tool for control, giving the narcissist control over the children.

One of the worst kinds of relationships will be when one narcissist turns another person into a narcissist. The possibility of healing the victim reduces to zero, and the narcissism plague will spread faster in their community. At first, the children born to narcissist parents may find it difficult to understand and appreciate things and people around them. Some may become bullies in school and try to intimidate other kids. Social areas like school and other social gatherings may help to restructure the child in understanding that the behavior being cultivated is not accepted by society, and they may seek to change.

During this change phase, the child in such a situation will eventually understand what agitates their parents, and what fulfills them. They may begin to behave like their parents due to a desire to obtain their love and affection because a narcissist cherishes seeing himself reflected in his children. They may also be destined to live a double life by concealing any character they may have that is not approved by their narcissist parents.

For instance, a narcissist parent openly struts with pride if the child has accomplished anything that is recognizable but will, however, demonstrate no further intrigue. The same parents will immediately feel humiliated by any sort of disappointment as a result of a failure by the child and will consistently ensure their children realize that they are hardly ever good enough.

The greatest ordeal for the children of narcissists will be to stay honest and true to themselves. It is usually not a simple childhood, not at any stage. It is extremely difficult to be a decent individual, especially if you have narcissistic parents because they are difficult to confide in. As children of narcissistic parents grew up with the line of thought that abuse, excessive love and admiration is necessary and the sole purpose of living, it may be difficult for other people to understand that the child is only doing what they learned from their narcissistic parents. As narcissist children succumb to bullying, other children may halt all forms of interaction and relationship with the narcissist child. This will make the narcissist child have very low self-esteem, thus affecting his method of interaction with other people and also showing signs of aggressive behaviors.

When a narcissist child notices that he or she has little or no form of relationship or bonding with other children or the general society, the child will be left in a dilemma to please his narcissist parents and to behave in an acceptable way in the society at the same time. Children of narcissist parents need to be showered with love and care and also to be taught how to interact with typical, well-functioning individuals instead of living all their lives to please their parents.

According to American Child Services, the average age a child will be considered to live on their own is within 16 to 18 years. Children within this age are normally kept with a caregiver (who is preferably their parent) or at home or orphanage. Invariably, this means that a child who stays with his narcissistic parents for 18 years has a higher chance of completely accepting the way of life of their narcissist parents. In the event that the child identifies that the character exhibited by the parents is not acceptable to the society, the child will most likely break contact with their parents with the hope that they need to get an opportunity when they become adults, but the options available to the child are very few as no one loves the idea of being with child services or in an orphanage.

It is usually difficult for these children to leave, and those who do, would need retribution, as the entire circumstance in which they grew is very out of line and disappointing. They have to feel engaged, and it can turn into a dangerous stance. However, with enough help, children of narcissists can turn out to be tolerant, well-adjusted grown-ups, who have the fundamental abilities to support others as well as themselves.

Narcissistic abuse is a variation of emotional and psychological abuse. It is primarily perpetrated by those who have either a Narcissistic Personality Disorder or an Antisocial Personality Disorder. Narcissism is the pursuit of gratification in a vain manner. It is the egocentric regard of one's self-image.

Narcissistic abuse also involves psychological and emotional abuse. You may feel like this is not your story because I mentioned abuse. You may assume you had a "normal" childhood. The question here is, what is the real definition of normal for you? Could it be growing up with the knowledge that good behavior equals love and affection and love only comes when you do exactly what is required of you? Or do you believe that you deserve the punishment you got as a result of your bad behavior?

Is your home filled with constant arguments, shouting, and verbal abuses? Has it been difficult to express your ideas without being looked down upon? Have your parents constantly lectured you that anything you need should be taken through deceit and by force? Did your parents constantly complain when you don't tell them how good they are? If the answers to these questions are positive or you are aware of someone who is going through this, the chances that they are living with parents who have narcissistic personality disorder is very high.

The Mayo Clinic has a very good description of narcissistic personality disorder. They define it as a mental condition where a person has an inflated sense of their reputation, an insatiable desire for admiration and attention, numerous troubled relationships, and a lack of empathy for others. Ring any bells? Does this remind you of your parents?

A lot of people live with the effects of a narcissistic parent or parents without knowing. Many have suffered and still do from the abuse and negative effect their narcissist parents had on them. They do not realize that they have been victims of a disorder and wonder why their lives are filled with so much negativity and depression. In this book, you will understand how the narcissistic behaviors of your parents can negatively affect you as an adult.

Many have suffered in silence. Many may wonder why growing up with their parents was such a nightmare and how they can escape the lingering effects of their upbringing on their adult life. The level of awareness about NPD before now has been low, and unfortunately, not much study has been conducted in regard. Statistics regarding this form of abuse, especially regarding its negative consequences on the parental relationship with children are hard to come by.

However, during my research, I came across some interesting statistics by Sandra L. Brown, founder of the Institute for Relational Harm Reduction and Public Pathology Education. Brown describes in her article titled *"60 Million Persons in the U.S. Negatively Affected by Someone Else's Pathology"* that of the 304 million people living in the US, 1 out of every 25 people will exhibit anti-social, sociopathic, and psychopath patterns – that's roughly 12.16 million people.

Millions of people are living with the after-effects of growing up in a narcissistic home. Ironically, many of these individuals have no idea that their parent or parents are narcissists and that they may have been negatively affected by the toxic behavior of their parent(s).

Living with a narcissistic parent is not a clear-cut situation, there's the possibility that you became the strongest among all the children. You eventually became the adult your parents couldn't live without. Or could it be that they projected an image of perfection? They had the final say in all matters that pertained to you, and your role was simply to obey or be punished by being shunned or affectively withheld. You may have had to struggle consistently with feelings of inadequacy and shame because your parents ridiculed you, tagging your efforts to reach individuality as rebellious.

This book provides a form of respite to your guilt-wracked soul by outlining exactly why the toxic behavior of your parents was never your fault. Your emotions may overwhelm you, causing you to think that the easiest way out is to walk away from your narcissist parents for good. Creating boundaries and developing a sense of self-worth helps in dealing with such parents. You sincerely love them and walking away from them because of their psychological disorder is not the best solution. Nevertheless, some questions beg for answers. Why is it that narcissistic abuse hasn't gotten as much public attention, awareness or research as it so desperately deserves? The fact is narcissism isn't really easy to spot because, unlike physical abuse, narcissistic abuse may not leave visible bruises or injuries. So many people live their lives without recognizing they have been abused because the effects of this abuse are also not usually noticed until after a very long time and when the damage has been done.

This book is projected to help you to better understand how to deal with narcissistic parents without walking away for good. It will expose you to virtually everything you need to know about narcissism, ranging from what goes on in the mind of a narcissist to talking about their ego, their selfishness, pride, and how they never see the views or pains of others.

This book will also help you understand who a narcissist parent is, as well as what are the narcissist parenting tendencies and symptoms. You will also learn about how a person becomes a narcissist parent. What the impact of narcissist parenting on children, teens, and adults is and how to proffer a solution. The aim of this book is to help as many people as possible to understand that hate is not the solution. It will also help everyone to accept and understand that narcissism is a psychological health problem that can be managed or cured. Most importantly, it will help you understand that you were not the problem as a child, but the influence your parents had on you might be a reason why you feel and behave the way you do. Finally, this book will help everyone understand the ways we can heal from the negative impact of narcissistic parenting.

1

The Mind of a Narcissist

W hat goes on in the mind of a narcissist? You may have been pondering this. What kind of thoughts could fuel the narcissist behavior? What is the rationale behind the actions of people with NPD, and why do they feel justified to let out their narcissism on others? Do they think normally like any other individual and still act differently? Do they think differently and consider anyone else to be strange?

If you have a narcissist parent or anyone with NPD around you, these thoughts, at one point of your life, could have crossed your mind. Just like no one knows what goes on in your mind except you, there are no techniques to magically figure out the things that go on in the mind of a narcissist. However, when we see a person with NPD, we could easily recognize them from their actions, behaviors, and omissions even when you are not able to figure out the reasons behind their actions.

The more we understand the behavior of persons with NPD, the more we can figure out their mindset. The more we understand all that constitutes a narcissist behavior, the better insight we would gain into the kind of mindset that shows the signs of NPD.

As earlier stated, Narcissistic Personality Disorder (NPD) is "a mental condition in which people have an inflated sense of their own importance, a deep need for excessive attention and admiration, many troubled relationships, and a lack of empathy for others. The deep and inflated sense of personal worth most times is ironically a mask beneath which lies a fragile self-esteem, that's vulnerable to the slightest criticism."

There are a whole lot of things that go on in the mind of every narcissist. Though, these signs may differ from person to person, here are a few highlights;

- People with NPD expect to get special treatment.
- They exaggerate their own smartness, success, power, and looks.
- Their lack of empathy leads them to take advantage of people, with no regrets.
- Narcissists may be tremendously envious and ultra-sensitive.
- They are very oversensitive, and they usually lash out furiously at any criticism or push-back.
- They may also lash out when they believe they are not getting special treatment.
- They are resistant to the everyday life experiences of setbacks and failures.

Beneath all these traits is a deep sense of insecurity. When all these traits are considered, there's no wonder why narcissists find it extremely taxing to have healthy relationships, and they have trouble interacting with people at work or school, in their friendships, and with their parents.

The narcissist usually has an exaggerated view of themselves. They are preoccupied with fantasies of unlimited success, and the unreasonable elevation of their capacity. The narcissist feels he should dominate and rule. Where there seems to be any objection to their self-bloated importance, it immediately causes friction in their relationship with others. Since the narcissist likes to see an extension of themselves in other people, at the beginning of their relationship a typical narcissist will usually idealize an attribute in relating to others.

This means that they want to recognize in other people that particular attribute that they assume to have themselves. For instance, where a person portrays the kind of success, the kind of dressing and manner of speaking which they think of as being the strong points they have themselves, they are attracted to such a person and are likely to fantasize and idealize him/her or have specific expectations towards him/her.

In cases where these expectations are not met, they resort to a destructive reaction. The person becomes worthless to their eyes and sometimes become violent. The narcissist is usually envious of people in his mind. His mind feels that they deserve what others have and even more. The level of envy in the mind of the narcissist makes it easy for him or her to be crafty in actions and very deceitful when in a relationship. A narcissist is quick to envy others and is full of hatred. Where they cannot dominate, rule, or control they become envious, and it develops into hate. Their lies act as a core foundation built on envy, and that usually forms the center of all their relationships.

There is a rising awareness about narcissist personality disorder and a corresponding rise in professional qualified persons who are being trained to help persons suffering from the effects of narcissist parents. However, this rise is far from the much-needed awareness, education, and help required to help the many thousands living with the cruel effect of narcissist parents. One of such people rising to provide help in the field of NPD is Margolis Felstead, Ph.D., LMFT who received her doctorate in Marriage and Family Therapy/Counselling from Oregon State University, and specializes in clients with narcissistic parents or spouses. Margolis, in one of her writing, points out the following signs as the common traits found in every narcissist.

It's not that easy to detect a narcissist as there are no physical medical processes – blood tests, MRIs, or X-rays that can be used to diagnose narcissism. Therapist must study behavioral patterns to determine if a person is a narcissist or not.

A lot of questions have been posed to psychologists about what exactly motivates a narcissist or what goes on in their mind. The question of how do you determine what goes on in the mind of a person, especially a person with NPD has been a topic over the decade for psychologists, and this is because what goes on in the mind of a person is not visible to any other person. Even though there are behaviors that are repeatedly seen as a constant pattern of how a human mind works, people with NPD have evolved to hide some repeated behaviors and devise new methods of expressing their inner need of care and excessive admiration.

You may have lived all your life with narcissist parents or family members without even thinking about the possibility for them to have a psychological disorder that could be managed if you understood it properly and also that you could have a better relationship with them. Instead, you have fought, resisted and always had a sour relationship with your parents because you did not agree with their style of parenting. Although some parents have a strict or harsh way of parenting, it doesn't mean that they are narcissists. They are only doing their best to make sure that a child doesn't follow the wrong path.

A narcissistic parent can only be identified by the child through constant observation and mind games. Mind games are simply when a child does a behavior repeatedly and predicts the response of the parent to the behavior. If the parent is constantly looking towards appreciation, love, and constant admiration without accepting any fault, then there are high chances that the parent is a narcissist. The way to know what goes on in the mind of a narcissist is to understand the behavior they exhibit. Their mindset and emotions result in the actions they take. Their mind propels their behavior, which results in the way they relate to the world.

Here is a list of all the symptoms and behaviors you should look out for to determine if a person suffers from narcissism. Note that not all of these have to be displayed to form a determination of narcissism. Concurring to the Demonstrative and Measurable Manual, which specialists utilize as a guide, an individual has to display at least 55% of the recognized characteristics to be considered narcissistic. The list made accessible hereunder is clear, so you will get a more in-depth picture of a narcissist's common behaviors.

1. *Superiority and privilege:* The world of the narcissist is about great/awful, unrivaled/sub-par, and right/wrong. There is a distinct progressive system, with the narcissist at the top, which is the main spot he has a sense of security. Narcissists must be the best, the most correct, the most skillful; they do everything their way, possess everything, and control everybody. Strangely enough, narcissists can also get that prevalent inclination by being the most exceedingly terrible, the most off-base, the most poorly steamed, or harmed for a while. At this point, they feel qualified to receive an alleviating concern and

reward and even request the privilege to hurt you or request expressions of remorse to "make things even."

2. *Overstated need for consideration and validation:*
Narcissists need consistent consideration at all times. They keep you busy around the house, requesting that you find things, or are always saying something to catch your attention. They have a deep need for approval.

A narcissist's requirement for approval can be compared to a funnel. You pour in positive, steady words, and they simply stream out the opposite end and are gone. For instance, you could begin from now until eternity to tell a narcissist you love them, respect them, or affirm them. They never feel they are good enough. Actually, they believe you adore and love them, but they do not believe that love and adoration are good enough or commensurate with their level or where they should be placed in your heart.

Regardless of all their self-retained, pretentious boasting, narcissists are, in reality, unreliable and dreadful; they do not have what it takes. They endeavor to get the commendation and support from others to support their delicate inner selves. Regardless of the amount of applause and endorsement they are showered with, they generally long for more.

3. **_Perfectionism:_** Narcissists have an incredibly significant requirement for everything to be immaculate. They think and believe they ought to be impeccable, they ought to be flawless, those occasions ought to happen exactly as they planned it, and life should play out decisively as they imagine it. This is obviously unattainable and can result in the narcissist feeling disappointed and miserable most of the time. The interest in flawlessness drives the narcissist to grumble and be continually disappointed.

4. **_Incredible need for control:_** Since narcissists are constantly disillusioned with the flawed way life unfolds, Narcissists can only achieve their objective when they seize emotional, financial, physical and psychological control over their victims. A narcissist's thirst for control is not usually noticed from the onset of any relationship with them. The control is developed gradually when they realize that their victim has complete trust in them and have no one else to turn to when a situation arises. Narcissists' desire for control is usually frustrating to them when they are not able to achieve it with their victim. Their desire for financial control is first seen when they willingly offer the victim financial assistance even before being asked. The narcissist victim develops a sense of gratitude and thinks that someone actually cares for him or her. The narcissist may repeatedly release the finances when the need arises.

After the victim has total confidence that the narcissist is always someone to rely on, the narcissist subsequently begins a backlash by constantly reminding the victim of how much has been given by them physically, emotionally, and otherwise. The victim's sense of constant gratitude, appreciation and the feeling that they can never be able to pay back the narcissist for all the love and kindness they have shown to them becomes a reality. This unending feeling of gratitude and appreciation makes the narcissist's sense of control to be almost permanent in the life of the victim.

Narcissists consistently have a storyline at the top of the priority list about what every "character" in their association ought to be saying and doing. When a narcissist notices that their schemes have been understood and recognized by the victim, they are quick to devise a story that will make the society see the victim of the narcissist as guilty or as an abuser. The narcissist will carefully take out scenes where the victim is confrontational or abusive and turn it to his own advantage in order to play the role of the victim. Their storylines are always coherent and will usually leave little or no traces for any other person to doubt their statements.

This storyline is always said to the people who hold the victim in high regard such as the victim's family, close friends and other relatives. The stories are also always said at the point when the victim doesn't behave as expected, which has led to the narcissist to become agitated. When the narcissist does not have a story to tell or when they don't have a clue as to what to expect since the victim has gone off course, they will request that the victim state and do precisely what they have at the top of their priority list so they can arrive at their ideal conclusion. You can be compared to a character in their well thought script and not a genuine individual with your very own thoughts and sentiments.

5. *Absence of obligation, blaming, and deflecting:* In spite of the fact that narcissists need to be in charge, they never need to be liable for the outcomes except if, obviously, everything goes precisely the way they want and the ideal outcome occurs. At the point when things don't go according to their arrangement, or they feel scrutinized or not exactly immaculate, the narcissist puts all the fault or blame on their victim. They believe this backdrop must be another person's shortcoming. On other occasions, the narcissist picks a specific individual or standard to blame anyone and anything that available to him, his mom, the judge, or the laws that limit what he needs to do. Be it as it may, the narcissist accuses the one individual who is genuinely close, steadfast, and cherished in his life and that person is the narcissist's victim. To keep up the façade of flawlessness, narcissists consistently need to accuse some other person or thing.

6. **Lack of limits:** Narcissists can't precisely observe where their person ends and when yours starts. They often behave like two-year-olds. They think that everything has its place and that everybody thinks and feels lesser than them. They also believe that everybody needs similar things as they do. They are stunned and exceptionally offended to be told otherwise. On the off chance that a narcissist needs something from you, he'll put everything on the line to make sense of how to get it through industriousness, cajoling, requesting, dismissing, or sulking.

7. **Lack of sympathy:** Narcissists have almost no capacity to relate to other people. They are, in general, narrow-minded and self-included and are typically unfit to comprehend what other individuals are feeling. Narcissists believe that others should think and feel the same way they do, and they are unwilling to understand how others feel. On a few occasions, they are conciliatory, contrite, or liable.

Be that as it may, narcissists are profoundly attuned to perceived danger, outrage, and rejection from others. Simultaneously, they lack in knowledge as regards the different sentiments of the individuals around them. Every now and then, they misread outward appearances that are not easily understood and interpret unclear outward appearances as a rejection of some sorts.

The narcissist is comfortable only in cases where you show your feelings significantly. A narcissist won't precisely experience what you are feeling, they only pretend to be emotionally attached. They have no sense of guilt or remorse. The narcissist is a good player when it comes to making others believe that he loves them and values them. He is quick to reaffirm his love for his victim, but he doesn't believe that the victim loves him; however, he is happy to hear the victim saying it repeatedly all over again.

The narcissist's repetition of the love he has for the victim may be doubted by the victim after the victim has witnessed several forms of abuse, control seeking nature and other different attitudes of the narcissist, therefore, the victim will always be doubting whatever the narcissist says whenever the narcissist is tense and furious. The narcissist may also have a hard time believing the victim and may even perceive any behavior of the victim or remarks as an assault.

Furthermore, if your words and articulations aren't consistent, the narcissist will probably react wrongly. This is the reason narcissists regularly misinterpret mockery. They see it as a genuine understanding or as an assault from other individuals. They lack the capacity to effectively pursue non-verbal communication; this is one reason why narcissists are inadequately sympathetic to your sentiments. They don't see them, they don't translate them effectively, and by and large, they don't think that you feel what they feel.

Likewise, narcissists have no idea how to interpret emotions. They do not see how their emotions develop. They think their sentiments are brought about by a person or thing outside of themselves. They don't understand that their emotions are brought about by their own natural chemistry, contemplations, and elucidations. Basically, narcissists consistently think you cause their sentiments, particularly the negative ones. They always think that since a victim does not fit into their expectations, the victim has to be blamed.

This lack of compassion makes genuine connections and enthusiastic associations with narcissists practically impossible. They simply do not see what any other individual is feeling.

8. **Weak emotional reasoning:** *On so many occasions, you* may have pondered on the reasons the narcissist behaves the way he does. You have probably tried to comprehend the agonizing impact of his behaviors on you. You imagine that in the case that he or she sees how much his conduct hurts you, they will change. The attempt to explain yourself, be that as it may, doesn't sound good to the narcissist, who just appears to be ready to defend himself about his own ideas and sentiments. Despite the fact that narcissists may say they understand, they genuinely don't.

For this reason, the accepted definition of a situation by a narcissist is dependent on how they feel about something. They believe they should have that green sport car, because of how they feel driving it, regardless of the fact that it could or could not be a thoughtful decision to make in relation with their family and their spending limit. On the off chance that they're exhausted or discouraged, they feel the need to move on or cut off the association or start another business. They generally look to a person or thing outside themselves to settle their emotions and necessities. They anticipate that you should oblige their "answers," and they respond with disturbance and hatred on the off chance that you do not.

9. **Parting:** The narcissist's character is divided into great and awful parts. They likewise split everything within their reach into great and terrible. Any negative considerations or practices are blamed on you or others, though they assume praise for everything that they do, that will surely be great. They deny their negative words and activities while consistently blaming you for objecting.

They also remember things as totally great and awesome or as awful and terrible. They cannot blend these two. Narcissists aren't ready to see, feel, or recollect both the positive and the negative in a circumstance. They can maintain just a single viewpoint at a time, and that will always remain the same.

10. **Fear:** The narcissist's whole life is spurred and stimulated by fear. Most of the narcissists' feelings of fear are profoundly covered and subdued. They are continually terrified of being belittled, rejected, or mistaken. They may have real fears about germs, about losing all their cash, about being genuinely or physically assaulted, about being viewed as terrible or insufficient, or about being relinquished. This makes it difficult for the narcissist to confide in any other individual because they have conflicting thoughts.

Actually, the closer your relationship becomes, the less he will confide in you. Narcissists dread any evident closeness or sense of powerlessness. They are afraid that you'll see their flaws and judge or reject them. No measure of consolation appears to have any kind of consoling effect on them. Narcissists profoundly detest and reject their own dishonorable defects. They can't stand their imperfections. Narcissists do not seem to trust in the adoration of others, and they persistently test you with more terrible and more awful behaviors in the attempt to discover your limit. Their apprehension over being "discovered" or relinquished never seems to diminish.

11. **Nervousness:** Nervousness is a progressing, dubious urge to feel that something awful is going on or about to occur. A few narcissists show their nervousness by speaking continually

about a fate that is going to occur, while some cover-up and subdue their tension. Yet, most narcissists blame their nervousness on their dearest friends and family, accusing them of being negative, unsupportive, rationally sick, not putting them first, not reacting to their needs, or being narrow-minded.

This move is intended to shift the tension they feel to the loved one and not trying to feel it themselves. As you feel more regret and guilt, the narcissist feels much improved and better. As a matter of fact, he feels more grounded and progressively predominant as you feel your uneasiness and depression grow.

12. **Disgrace:** Narcissists don't feel a lot of blame. They believe they are right in every situation. They don't accept they are at fault and exhibit behaviors that truly influence other individuals. In any case, they harbor a ton of disgrace. Shame is the conviction that there is something profoundly wrong or awful about who you are.

The narcissist is filled with insecurities, fears, and dismissed attributes. As such, he is continually on the lookout to avoid anybody, including himself. The narcissist covers in a false sense of self. He keeps all his vulnerabilities hidden because he is intensely embarrassed about all these faults. Eventually, in any case, this makes it inconceivable for him to be totally genuine and straightforward.

13. **_Insensitive:_** On account of their lack of sympathy, and a consistent need for self-glorification, narcissists can't genuinely cherish or interface sincerely with other individuals. They can't take a look at the world from any other person's point of view – that's simply impossible. They are genuinely visually impaired and alone, which makes them sincerely emotionally impoverished. No matter how hard you try, a narcissist is wired to see things in their own perspective and cannot be convinced otherwise.

When a relationship is no longer as fulfilling as they expect it to be, the Narcissist starts another one at the earliest opportunity. A narcissist doesn't really end the previous relationship by himself. He tries to subdue the victim to believe that they are still needed, loved, and wanted. The narcissist makes the victim believe that the reason why they would like to move on is because of what the victim has done to them or what the victim cannot provide for them. This keeps the victim in a self-blame phase where they feel that they are not capable of taking care of a man, and therefore they need the support of the narcissist to learn the basic requirements to take care of a man.

When the victim feels like this, the narcissist has successfully reversed the victim's mindset while he claims to be the victim, and the real victim becomes the abuser. The narcissist does this because they frantically need somebody to sympathize with their agony, to identify with them, and to make everything exactly as they need it to be. Be that as it may, they have little capability to react to your torment, fear, or even your everyday need for care and compassion.

14. ***An inability to present oneself or fill in as a major element of a group:*** It is terribly difficult when a person doesn't understand other people in a group or show empathy or care to a group of people. Narcissists lack empathy and are not ready to let other people feel like they are deserving of care and love. In some business environments where narcissists are bosses or supervisors, it is difficult to see their team abilities as they are domineering and cannot seem to find a way to let others express themselves or voice their own opinion. Attentive, helpful behaviors require a genuine understanding of other's feelings. An empathic person asks him/her self how will the other individual feel? Will this activity fulfill both of us? In what way will this influence our relationship? These are questions that narcissists don't have the ability or the inspiration to consider. Do not expect that the narcissist can understand your emotions, and may yield, or quit all pretenses; it is futile. He needs to be in an advantaged position.

The narcissist mind is full of means and ways to make his victim feel loved and cared for before enacting any form of abuse. The narcissist's parent is somewhat the same and never ceases to constantly desire appreciation and incessant love and care from their children. The narcissistic parent is no different from the typical narcissist depicted above, as the level of admiration, love, and other behaviors expected from their children is very high while the level of love and care they show to their children is unequal to what they are expecting.

2

Narcissist Parenting

A narcissistic parent is a parent that has narcissism personality disorder or has a narcissistic character. The traits, emotions, and behaviors specific to narcissists are generally seen in them. Also, they may be able to lead their children to behave like them, or they abuse their children who refuse to behave like them.

Narcissistic parents are able to do this because they are the only in charge of their kids. They undermine their children's growing autonomy. The outcome is a narcissistic relationship, with the parent thinking that the child exists exclusively to satisfy the parent's needs and wishes.

When the narcissist young victim refuses to be like their parent, the parent frequently resorts to threats and psychological abuse to control their children. Narcissistic child-rearing negatively influences the mental development of kids. It wrongly influences their thinking, their enthusiastic morale, and cultural practices as well as dampens their frame of mind. Individual limits are frequently disregarded with the objective of trimming and controlling the child to fulfill the parent's desires.

Narcissistic individuals have a low level of confidence. They want to control how others respect them; if they fail in being respected, they could be accused or rejected, and their own deficiencies would be discovered. Narcissistic parents are self-assimilated, frequently to the point of being pompous. They are strong-willed, unyielding and short of the compassion, essential for child-raising.

The word "narcissism," as used in Sigmund Freud's clinical examination, incorporates behaviors such as self-glorification, confidence, weakness, fear of losing the friendship of particular individuals, fear of disappointment, fear of dependence on some defined mechanisms, compulsiveness, and interpersonal conflict.

To keep up their confidence and secure their powerless genuine selves, narcissists look to control the conduct of others, especially that of their children whom they see as extensions of themselves. Consequently, narcissistic parents may talk about "leading" and keeping up the family representation, or making mother or father proud. They may censure their kids for displaying shortcomings, being excessively emotional, being childish, or not meeting expectations. Some narcissistic parents can inflict physical wounds on their children because they believe that their children need to understand the reasons behind their decisions.

Children of narcissist parents eventually figure out how to wield their influence and flaunt their uncommon skill(s), particularly on other people. They do not have numerous memories of having felt loved or acknowledged for acting naturally, rather, they connect their experience of love and gratefulness with fitting in the requests and needs of the narcissistic parent.

Destructive narcissistic parents have this pattern; to be the focal point of consideration, they always look compliments, put down their kids consistently, and make sure that their kids' self-esteem is low with the hope that their kids will look up to them as a shield for high self-esteem. Discipline is used to find fault, analyze short-comings, or as emotional blackmail. This system might be utilized to guarantee consistency with the parent's desires.

What really makes a parent a narcissist?

According to the Mayo Clinic, no one truly knows the precise causes of this disorder in parents. It regularly begins to appear in adolescence and early adulthood, and the components that lead to it are no doubt complex. It is most likely a combination of genetics, neurobiology (which means how the brain is connected and how it influences conduct and thinking), and condition (the manner in which the individual was raised). Invariably, the chances of a parent being raised from childhood to adulthood by a narcissist parent will determine if the narcissist will also raise their child in the same manner. This is because they are used to that form of tough love, care, and abuse and have seen it as a normal way of life. American Psychology statistics says that out of every 3 narcissist parents, only one child has a chance of escaping the abuse and treatment of their parent with the intention of living a life that is far different from what their parents practiced and introduce them to.

This one child that escapes the narcissist parent may still have very low self-esteem for some years in their life; however, they end up being the ones that teach other children about how to deal with narcissistic parents and how to break free from them.

The impact of narcissist parenting on children, teens, and adults

Narcissism will, in general, play out intergenerationally, with narcissistic parents producing either narcissistic or co-narcissistic children. While a self-assured or sufficient parent can permit their child to proceed on their self-governing advancement, the narcissistic parent may rather utilize the kid to advance their own image. A parent worried about self-improvement, or with being reflected and respected by their kid, may leave the kid feeling like a mannequin to their parent's emotional/scholarly requests.

Children of a narcissistic parent may not be accommodating of others in their home. Observing the conduct of the parent, the child discovers that control and blame are successful methods that can be used to ensure you ignore what the other person needs. These children may develop a fake version of their true selves and use animosity or intimidation to get their way.

However, not all children of narcissists become forceful, phony, manipulative grown-ups. Some of them may decide to channel their energy and resources into contrary practices they may have observed as they watched their companions and different families. At some point when the children of a narcissistic parent encounter shelter, genuine love and care or see it conveyed or shown by other parents in other families, they may understand the difference between narcissistic love and real love. They may compare their parents to the family they admire or try to challenge their narcissist parents with examples of the families whose parenting style they admire. They may also decide to learn and absorb the values that differ between their life and that of a child in a solid family.

For instance, the lack of sympathy and unpredictability at home may build the child's own compassion and need to be respectful. Correspondingly, having an intense or extreme need for control and a lack of regard for boundaries at home may build the child's incentive for understanding others and their longing to extend affection to other people.

In spite of the fact that the child observes the parent's conduct, they are regularly on the lookout for better examples to emulate rather than ending up behaving like their parents. At some point when an option that differs from the constant agony and misery that is being caused at home presents itself, the child may decide to concentrate on all the consoling and affectionate initiating behaviors.

Some normal occurrences in narcissistic child-rearing are a result of the absence of proper, mindful nurturing. This may leave a child feeling unfulfilled, worried about the future, uncertain about relationships that involve love and romance, being doubtful of others, and standing a failure to achieve a specific goal because it is the result expected by their parent.

Over the years, there are a lot of emotionally delicate children who have had unimaginable low self-esteem that makes them live a life filled with self-blame, and their families can't seem to figure out how to address their parents' needs for satisfaction. They search out ways they can fulfill the desires of their parents and receive the love they crave. The child's ordinary emotions are disregarded, denied and in the long-run subdued in endeavors to pick up the parent's "affection."

Constant self-blame, a feeling of shame and disgrace, can keep the child locked in a developmental halt. Other forceful driving forces such as wrath may cause the child to become divided into personality and to fail to develop a unitary self. A few children born to narcissist parents and trying to escape the grips of their narcissist parents may develop a fake personality and prefer to be seen as someone else. They may claim that their parents have abandoned them, have died, or have been locked up in a secured prison. The reason behind this disassociation and claims is to avoid being judged by other people or avoid their behaviors being linked to their parents that is probably well known to be a narcissist.

In some cases, the child may not be aware of disowning their actual and true selves or their birth parents, but they just feel more comfortable adjusting to the new life that has been presented to them. It may cause them to sustain a cycle of self-loathe, and they constantly dread any reminder of their true selves.

The child may not want to mention anyone or anything that can make other people trace their lineage, home, or the community they grew up in. Fake identities may be gotten and a complete change of name, hair color, and body movement, all in the attempt to totally disassociate any link or connection to their narcissist parents.

On the other hand, when the narcissist child could not gain acceptance to any community after leaving the parents, they may decide to flow with the tide by accepting any other negative association or friends just to get by each day. This may encourage the child to take all sorts of threats or danger, sexual addiction, misuse of medications or liquor, and acting out in a possibly unsafe way to gain attention. The American Society of Psychologists conducted a research in 2005 and was of the opinion that many women involved in prostitution are not necessarily enjoying such behaviors. They have been raised by narcissist parents and in the attempt to start a new life or run away from home, became victims of gangs that have led them into prostitution. The research suggests that, although these narcissist children are not happy with their trade as prostitutes, they have accepted that it is the only trade that can provide finances for their survival.

Some narcissist children who leave their homes as teens without any formal education, help, direction, love, and support from well-meaning friends grow up feeling molested, abused, and with extremely low self-esteem. When they become teens, they may change their line of trade to something much worse, all with the sole intention of surviving.

Over a few years, some narcissist teens may perfect their trade in the area they have practiced over the years and therefore raise another group of narcissist children to join their trade. Across various prisons in America and Africa, almost all the stories of inmates suggest that they are from narcissist homes, and they strongly believe that their method of survival is the only method available for them. This accounts for the reason why the American Association of psychologists says that one out of every three convicted felon who was raised by a narcissist parent and has been set free to live their normal life; at least one of the ex-convicts will return to continue the act that got them convicted previously. These narcissist children, once turned into adults may be blamed for their choice by the society; however, upon proper investigation, it would be seen that the narcissist develops such behavior from their narcissist parents or when the child left the narcissist parents and began a relationship with bad friends.

Effects of narcissistic parenting

Because of their helplessness, children are extremely influenced by the conduct of a narcissistic parent. A narcissistic parent has the habit of handling their children in a rough manner. They play the typical parental role of "director" of their children. They are the fundamental decision-maker in the child's life and end up excessively possessive and controlling. This possessiveness and inordinate control weaken the child; the parent sees the child essentially as an extension of themselves. This may have a negative influence on the child's creative mind and decrease their level of interest, instead of a regular build-up of a lifestyle of inspiration. This degree of control might be caused by the need of the narcissistic parent to keep the child's reliance on them.

Narcissistic parents get angry easily; they may put their children in danger of physical and psychological abuse. To avoid being the object of their parent's fury, children of narcissistic parents always agree to all of their parent's request whether the request is a good one or a bad one. Some narcissists and sadistic parents can train and engage their children in any act that can prove irrespective of any laws that prohibit child labor. As such, children of narcissistic parents lack the ability to make legitimate choices on their own because they've been told what to do their entire lives. As grown-ups, they are always in need of self-assurance and lack the capacity to deal with an intense life that is not beneficial to their family. This is very possible for the narcissistic parent to achieve because children are usually loyal to their parents, especially at a young age. Growing up with undivided loyalty and trust for their narcissist parents makes it almost impossible to correct the negative influences that the narcissist parent has in the life of the child.

Children of narcissistic parents often battle with an identity crisis, depression, and self-articulation. The struggle to find one's self as a grown-up stems from the notably frequent occurrence of the unconscious transfer of their parent's desires experienced as a kid. Due to the continued acceptance of their parent's desires, the child may never get the chance to explore their very own identity. A part of these occurrences is blamed on the culture of our society.

Most people believe that a child should be obedient to their parents, respect them, love them and not question their decisions as it is the best decision for a good life and to be accepted in society. However, people will hardly monitor what the narcissist parent is actually doing to their child. They believe that everything is fine when the child doesn't complain and sometimes use narcissist children as an example to their own children. Although it is applaudable when a child's love, loyalty, and care is to his parents and for the well-being of the society, it is also important to be very observant and ask specific questions when the child tries to take a stand against the behavior or abuse of their narcissist parents in public. This singular act may reduce the chances of a narcissist child growing up with a narcissistic parent and spreading the plague of narcissism throughout the world.

Several studies have shown that children of narcissistic parents have fundamentally higher levels of discouragement and lower self-confidence in adulthood than the individuals who didn't have narcissistic parents. A narcissist parent's lack of sympathy towards their children adds to this, as the child's desires are frequently denied, their sentiments limited, and their general emotional wellbeing overlooked, they end up accepting the idea that they do not deserve anything good and even if they do deserve it, it must be gotten through forceful means.

The use of force as the only available option makes the narcissist children hide their low self-esteem, which will be frowned at by those whom they want to express how superior they are to them. This action is interpreted as bullying by a lot of people; however, it is only an escape of the image of the little child that is within.

Children of narcissistic parents have been taught to submit and adjust, making them lose contact with themselves as individuals. This will prevent the child from having many memories or feelings of being acknowledged or loved for being true as they would rather associate the love and gratefulness by agreeing to everything their parents want.

A lot of children, whether born to a narcissist parent or not, will profit from some level of reasonable distance from any narcissistic parent. A few children of narcissistic parents resort to venturing out from home during puberty as they grow and understand that their association with either of their parents or both of them are toxic to their life and mindset.

In addition, based on the reactions and responses of a lot of people on the different online platforms on narcissism, it is evident that there are hundreds of thousands of people across the world who were raised by at least one narcissist. This has wreaked havoc on their self-esteem, their feelings of well-being and safety, and their certainty and boldness. Being raised by a narcissist gives rise to a belief throughout our lives that we are just not "good enough" in spite of everything we try to achieve and bending over with the unending hope to please others.

Another challenging factor is that more children raised by a narcissist have no idea how to set boundaries about them, especially after being influenced by the narcissist parent. They are used to do whatever their parents ask them, regardless of how they feel about it. As adults, they find it difficult to set boundaries and are often taken advantage of by others. They have no idea what they can tolerate and what they loathe. Thus, they lack the capacity to communicate perfectly and effectively, and the ability to flourish in the world has been tampered with.

Most grown-up children of narcissists never get the assistance they so require to recover and heal. This is because they have no clue about what they have encountered as children; thus, they feel they are undesirable and become destructive to other people and the general society. They live a very disconnected and unsociable life and can go on with the rest of their lives without even realizing there's a problem.

On a personal level, I have had a fair share of individual experience with narcissism for a very long time. I can tell you beyond a shadow of a doubt that if perhaps you were raised by a narcissist parent, your boundaries are not what you imagine them to be. You need to recover and heal and become a person who understands their personality and is said to be solid, upbeat, and sure. You need to face life head-on and gain experience from this.

Being a marriage and family counsellor, I saw first-hand that grown-up children of narcissists can live their whole lives believing they are not good enough, and looking for approval or acknowledgment every step of the way, yet never feeling like they have received it, except once they receive the help that they obviously need to recover and defeat it.

Expectedly, children of narcissists are excessively delicate, profoundly shaky, unfit to consider themselves to be great, commendable, and lovable. Unfortunately, they become used to narcissism, and this is because they have endured the torture and all the experiences from a narcissist for their entire lives, and unknowingly it becomes a lifestyle that affects their grown-up relationships, their work culture, and professions.

The interesting fact to note with narcissist parents is that they do not always shower love, care, and attention on their children in the attempt to make their children their victim. Narcissistic parents usually want to get their supply from other sources, which they can easily disengage when they feel they need to find another source of supply.

Narcissist parents are usually very mean to their children, without showing any form of love, care, empathy, or affection towards their children. Narcissistic parents can be deemed as pure sadists because they may behave as though the child is not theirs. However, when the child reacts to the abuse and lack of affection from the parent, the narcissist becomes more aggressive, defensive, and resorts to threats that can change the life of the child for a very long time.

The narcissist parent may constantly leave their current relationship for new ones, which keeps changing the life and social being of the child throughout childhood and teenage years. The worst kind of narcissism parenting is when both parents are narcissists or, one narcissist parent has succeeded in converting their partner to become a narcissist. This makes it almost impossible for any child to thrive or grow in that environment or succeed later on with their life ambitions.

A considerable number of persons have suddenly realized that they were brought up in a narcissist environment, and now understand why their careers and individual struggles can be traced right back to what they learned as children of narcissists while growing up.

A Narcissistic Personality Disorder disrupts several parts of our lives, and as a result, our relationships at work, school or monetary undertakings can be adversely affected. You might realize you are troubled or baffled when you are not given the exceptional favors or profound respect you believe you deserve.

Others may not appreciate being around you, and you may discover your relationships are unfulfilling.

New studies have demonstrated that 6% of the population has encountered clinical NPD (Narcissistic Personality Disorder) at one point or the other in their lives. Yet, a lot more encounter non-clinical indications.

From personal research, I strongly believe that narcissism is definitely more common than we are aware of, and we all are surrounded by grown-up children of narcissists. Yet these adults have no idea of it they don't have any acquaintance with it or remember it since they are uninformed about this disorder or somehow happen to catch wind of it in the ordinary course of their lives.

There is a lot to state about the destructive impacts of narcissism, yet I would like to focus on how it impacts us in our vocations. The following are the characteristics and signs that you may have been raised by a narcissist, and your lifestyle has been influenced by this. Yet, I have to share that it is basic for your prosperity that you don't turn around and start accusing (or despising) your parents if they are/were narcissists. The fact is that most narcissist parents were raised by narcissists, and the way you've been treated is likely to come from their own harmful childhood or adolescence that needed healing, which they never got.

So, we are not accusing anyone; however, we want to provide an insight into this fundamental issue so that on the off chance that you have being raised by a narcissist, you can understand what the issues are, get some assistance, and explore the difficulties effectively.

I've learned also that narcissistic parents demand that you agree with them; otherwise, they will reject you. They interpret being challenged as not being loved. In this way, grown-up children of narcissists only experience love that is conditional, based on the specific conditions and explicit actions that must be demonstrated before they can receive love. From experience, they must have a specific goal to be accomplished before they can be loved or acknowledged. They never get the approval, compassion, and unconditional love and support that we all crave for.

Here are a few things adult children of narcissists often feel:

- Never adequate or significant enough.
- Profoundly scared to speak up with confidence or challenge others.
- Very adjusted (to a more or less uncanny degree) to what everyone around them is feeling since they possess a hypersensitivity to what other people are experiencing (they needed to have this so as to endure being raised by

a narcissist). This can lead to their incapability to shield themselves from others' feelings.

- Constantly uncertain of themselves, and excessively stressed by how others consider them.
- Profoundly shaky, as a result of the fact that they never experienced unequivocal love. Any love or care that was given was done under certain difficult conditions that made them feel inauthentic and counterfeit.
- The relationships they've created either at work or in their personal lives are deeply challenging, unacceptable, terrifying, and even toxic. When they reflect on this relationships, later on, they realize they had attracted the wrong crowd.

In light of this, if the experiences highlighted above match with yours, then it's time to gain a better awareness of what you've passed through as a little child whilst growing up, so you can have a better understanding of your thoughts, behaviors, and mindsets in order to heal properly.

One thing caused by being raised by a narcissist is the fact that we don't just "get over" it. It takes serious therapeutic assistance and help to heal the wounds, to have the boldness to look at the precise kind of narcissism you personally experienced (because it varies in every family), how these experiences have affected you and the way and manner you function and learn innovative behaviors that will help you to heal the child within and turn out to become the adult you desire to be.

The problem with narcissistic parents

Recently, a study by Stress in America revealed that Millennials (ages 18 to 33) reported the most noteworthy stress levels of any age. It's not really wrong to credit these stress-related burdens to increasing challenges at school and the work environment, a weak economy, or a culture adopted for multitasking. However, let us consider something more personal that might be the origin of increased stress levels.

How narcissistic parents live through their children

Parents who put up a show by immersing themselves in their kid's interests, activities, and accomplishments, are habitually taking more than they are giving. Narcissistic parents, many times feed their own ego through the successes of their children. In spite of the fact that this behavioral pattern is, to some degree, an unconscious act, they seek out ways they can live through their children.

The art of living through their child is done in a very simple way. Most unsuccessful narcissistic parents who were not able to make a social name for their family, live through their children by claiming that they are pushing the child to be the best that they can be. Assuming a narcissist parent was not able to obtain a college degree or become a professional in a certain field of study, they will make sure that they do all they can for their child to achieve what they were not able to attain. They can become abusive or even decide to starve the child of food and other social amenities because they feel that all forms of distraction have to be eliminated before the child can succeed.

For example, if a narcissist parent who always wanted to be an accountant finds that it is not possible for them to achieve their professional dream anymore, they can insist that their child must be an accountant by putting the child in an accounting school. In most cases, the child has no dreams of being an accountant or even hates numbers and calculations. The narcissist parent increases this mental torture by constantly reminding the child that they can never achieve anything good in life if they do not take the accounting classes seriously.

To the public and close friends, they may view the child as being stubborn or not wanting to have a good future and see the parent as the victim. When the child succumbs to the decision of the parent by following the dreams of their narcissist parent, the child ends up living a life of regret because that is not the passion of the child. As the child keeps living a life of regret waiting for a day to be set free, the narcissistic parent capitalizes on the success of the child and flaunts the image of the success for the general public to applaud and appreciate their level of persistence and control over their child. They may use their child as an example to other parents, and all this is done without the happiness of the child being considered.

Why narcissistic parents overly connect to their children

Narcissistic parents crave their child's performance to directly reflect on them. The reason behind this is mind-boggling. Parents might attempt to make up for what they accept is their own inadequacies. They may rely on their child's success to bolster themselves up. In doing so, they are failing to see their child as a unique and autonomous individual.

They don't perceive that their child is an individual with their own thoughts, sentiments, and wants. A narcissistic parent will, in general, seek the spotlight or practically "feed" off their child's achievements. They do this all the time because they have this void within them. They may attempt to make use of their children to fill this void. Parents living rich and full lives have countless interests, close relationships, and passions, and often give more to their children than those who give up everything to be with their kids.

In spite of the fact that they do this for the sake of affection, they don't understand that their idea of love is really wrong. People frequently mistake love for emotional craving. Parents who think they are giving their children love by showering them with constant attention fail to see how much they are holding on to or draining the child. At some point, when an individual feels a "need" or "aching" for their kid, it may very well be a warning that they are taking more than they are giving in the relationship.

Narcissist parents do not only connect to their children because of the void they feel inside them, but they can also do this because they are obsessed with love for their children. Although this is natural to many parents, especially mothers, it will be difficult to establish the baseline for this connection as it is inborn within them. Scientists say that when a mother's fetus is attached to the umbilical cord, the baby feeds from the mother, feels most of what the mother is feeling, and even respond to sounds and touches from the mother. This has made it very easy for a natural bond, love, loyalty, and understanding to be established.

For the narcissist fathers, the connection and love are present when they are the biological father of the child. It may be termed as mother nature's own way of making the family united. However, when it comes to narcissist parents, their connection to their child is very unique. It is almost impossible for the child of a narcissist to disobey their parent. The disobedience is seen after repeated abuse or when the narcissist child decides it is time to move away from the family.

On the off chance that a parent feels their kid is "filling up" a part of them, for instance, that they are their sole source of happiness, it may very well be another caution that they are demanding more than is necessary emotionally from their child. Love is an offering of encouragement, support, and fondness. Emotional hunger, on the other side, provides just the exact opposite.

The effects of being raised by narcissistic parents

The greatest challenge we encounter when we grow up with narcissistic parents is that, in an attempt to develop their children as they grow up, they are actually failing to perceive and boost their child's independent feeling of self. Rather, what the child feels is a serious amount of pressure from their parents. They are burdened by the fears of falling short of their parent's expectations and become filled with the belief that they will never be good enough. Their self-esteem becomes very low, and depression may set in. In most cases, the person who can help cure the feeling of depression of a narcissist child is usually the parent of the child, and this also accounts for the deep connection that exists between the parents.

However, their weaknesses may cause them to eventually end up as narcissists themselves because they are in constant search for appreciation, love, applaud, and endorsement before they can feel good about themselves once again. Parents who give up their own lives and plunge themselves into the life of their child instead of inviting the child into theirs are narcissists.

Every person has their own life to live, and after some years, everyone is capable of making their own decisions. Parents often feel that they are responsible for the decision or the life of their child and this makes them keeping pushing even if the child is saying "no" and refusing all forms of control. The narcissist parent may insist on being involved with every event in their child's life, and this includes style of clothing, friends, and even take over wedding plans if possible.

When children notice that their parents don't feel fulfilled, they tend to blame themselves and actually do all they can to help their parents feel better. This isn't a burden a child should experience and definitely not one they can handle. They may reproduce this pattern in their connections, searching for somebody who blows up their inner self or who tears them down in manners that help the deep-seated frames of mind they have toward themselves. They may also search out individuals who are similar to their parents, and use them to feel better about themselves.

These dynamics can be damaging to an adult, but they are almost immoral and inhumane to impose such on a little child. When we fail to see our children as separate individuals, we project all of the negative and critical attitudes we have towards ourselves onto them. We may try to overcompensate for our parents' mistakes, or we may re-enact negative models from our own childhoods.

In either case, we are missing the mark with our children. We are not attuned to their distinctive desires, and we become insensitive to their true wants. By differentiating from our own past, we are better able to see our children as separate from ourselves. Only then can we offer them real love as opposed to a fantasy of connection, and only then, can we appreciate our children for who they really are and support them in reaching their full, distinctive potential.

Many parents have become narcissist over the years because they were trying to fulfill their dreams in the life of their child in a very inappropriate way. Some can be so abusive in other to exercise full control over their children. All this is done without considering the effect it will have on the children presently and in the future, such as making their child develop very low self-esteem, making their child grow up believing that they can't make decisions for themselves, initiating depression and even turning the child to be a narcissist. Although most parents do this in good faith, they may not know when they are going off-track, and the repercussions are always very serious.

If only all parents realized that they are responsible for bringing the child to the world but not responsible for making all their life decisions, there would be fewer narcissist parents to deal with.

3

Problems Associated with Narcissistic Parenting

W hether we like it or not, who we are today is the reflection of our childhood experiences, and our decisions in time, past and present behaviors are a direct result of our upbringing. Several individuals have cheerful and healthy childhoods, which enable them to grow up as well-adjusted and wholly functional individuals.

There are many problems that are linked to narcissistic parenting, and these problems are mostly psychological or the result of their need for social status. The psychological problems that have made narcissist parents behave the way they do are not far-fetched. Parents who have had lots of pressure and various demands from their family, society and workplace can be going through some psychological changes. For example, if the pressure is caused by the kind of work they do, their mind can make them feel that they need their children to be as strong as they are or as bold as they are.

Parents who are not able to cope with the mental pressure that comes from their work environment can resort to drugs for stability to reduce stress levels. Although stress levels can be controlled through medication, there are chances that the parent will not be fully relieved of the challenges and stress that come from their demanding jobs. Parents like this will channel their anger, frustration, and hate towards their children. This psychological effect will lead to constant use of negative languages, and also bring about an attitude to show their child that they cannot beat their level of success or performance in any area of their life.

A child who is constantly going through this mental torture keeps struggling to reach the heights their parents are with the hope that it will bring some form of love, attention, and admiration from their parents. The child will have no other option than to find ways to please their parents because their parents control the finances, the groceries, the shelter, and almost everything that concerns them. Narcissist children often tend to be narcissists themselves because their ability to control or take charge of things that concern their life and living is very limited.

In any case, sadly, not every person is equally happy. When we were younger, our critical reasoning skills were still evolving. This implies that as children, we gain knowledge from what we see and hear. What's more, in the event that you were raised by narcissists, then you may have some intense psychological issue you are managing as an adult.

At first, you may feel that there is no way you could have been raised by narcissistic parents. Be that as it may, this sort of childhood experience may be more delicate than you might have suspected.

Signs that would have been effectively recognizable would have been difficult to figure out and understand as a child. How could you have known if either or both your parents were narcissists or covert narcissists? Here are a few questions that would help in determining that. Were your parents/guardians:

- Irrationally and particularly domineering of you?
- More often than not, engaging in marginalized competition with you?
- Scared or apprehensive about your independence?
- Constantly casting you inside their shadows?
- Constantly having unrealistic expectations, you can't ever seem to reach?

You were doubtlessly raised by narcissists if the answers to these questions above are yes. In retrospect, there is one simple identifiable sign, which is this; if you have always pretty much felt that they couldn't love you for who you are.

Nevertheless, you can argue that the majority of parents are only being protective. As a matter of fact, quite a number of parents put these pressures on us so as to make us perform at our very best because they want us to succeed, and many parents show us off when we achieve something to make them proud.

All of these things, however, don't essentially imply they have narcissistic tendencies. What differentiates a narcissistic parent is their increasingly-existing predisposition to refuse their children their own identity. It is their "conditional" love that actually turns them into narcissists, and their unflinching need to take away their child's sense of "self."

Two types of narcissistic parents

Narcissism is displayed in diverse ways. In parents, however, there are two fundamental types of narcissism;

1. Ignoring narcissists: Some narcissistic parents are so self-absorbed that they end up neglecting their children. Narcissistic parents who are regarded as ignoring narcissists are the parents who show almost no enthusiasm in their children's lives. They see their kids as a threat or an inconvenience and as such, intentionally decide not to make an effort to improve their childhood. Parents like these are usually successful and have a very high public profile. Ignoring Narcissist parents also do their best to maintain the attention of the public by always taking family pictures, going to venues or events where they will be seen in the eyes of the public and admired as the perfect family.

Ignoring narcissists always threaten their child or punish them when they do not behave or speak well of them in public. Unfortunately, they may also say negative things about their child when the child decides to voice out or create doubts about their poor parenting skills in public. Just like a narcissist, the blame game and playing the victim game is an easy thing for an ignoring narcissist parent. The society automatically sides with the narcissistic parent when they are playing the victim game for two main reasons. The first is that they are the parent, working hard to provide for the child, and secondly, children are always known to be difficult to raise, control or care for. Many narcissist parents who ignore their children are good actors. They can cry in front of the camera or take pills in front of the camera just to get sympathy, love, and appreciation about how bad the child has turned out to be.

2. *Engulfing narcissists:* This is a direct opposite of ignoring narcissists. The engulfing narcissistic parents display a fanatical inclusion in their children's lives. They consider their children as a major part of their very own selves. In doing this, they enforce their very own character and identity on their children and become disappointed when they veer off from it. These sorts of parents don't have limits and have serious challenges separating themselves from their kids. The engulfing narcissistic parent is not usually as dramatic as the ignoring narcissist parent. The good quality of this narcissist parent is that in their mind, they are actually doing their best for their child without knowing they have turned to narcissists.

The engulfing narcissist tries hard to make the child attain what they would have loved to attain but for one reason or the other, never made it into that class of society. The disadvantage of an engulfing narcissist is that they do not allow their children to express their feelings, emotions or having a voice about the kind of life that would make them happy. They are called engulfing narcissists because their behavior is usually targeted at one goal which is to create their own happiness by destroying another person's dreams.

Engulfing narcissists are also more stubborn, self-willed, and love excessive control of their victims. Their insistence on making their children follow their own desired path is coerced by their desire for social status. Engulfers are also known to be abusive both secretly and in public, unlike the ignoring narcissist. The level of abuse and insults rained on their children is usually done openly to increase the possibility of their child's decision to their favor. However, the engulfing narcissists and the ignoring narcissists have some things in common. These are their desire to gain love, admiration, acceptance, respect, care and exercise control of their victim; that is, their child.

From a therapist's perspective

Lots of therapists deal with patients who suffer from being raised by a narcissist. An author, life coach and a licensed family therapist, Kathy Carpino, has definitely dealt with her own share, as she says;

"I saw first-hand that adult children of narcissists can't live a whole life unless they get help to heal and overcome the thinking that they are not good enough, and seeking validation and recognition at every turn, yet never feeling they get it."

Can a narcissist be a good parent?

As discussed earlier, narcissists who become parents respond in two different ways, which are; ignoring or engulfing narcissistic parents. Be that as it may, is there an exception to the rule? Is there a possibility for a narcissist to be a good parent?

With the two kinds of behaviors, you can see an indispensable characteristic – disconnection. Looking at it carefully, even the engulfing narcissistic parent is emotionally depressed, lacks warmth and security, and is constantly separated from love, wholeness, and to some extent, from society. The separation from society is stronger when the child has failed to attain a new level in their careers or success story as quickly as their counterparts.

Tragically, there is scarcely any research and no official studies to give a clear-cut answer to this question. That is not to say that experts do not have their hypotheses, though.

According to Ramani Dracula, who is the author of *Surviving a Relationship with a Narcissist,* and *Should I Stay or Should I Go?* "Narcissistic parents beget kids with a whole host of psychological problems. One thing I can guarantee you is that children of narcissists will be plagued by doubt and insecurity for the rest of their lives. The question is how that is going to manifest."

People with high levels of insecurity emit a very strong emotion that everyone who wants to enter into a relationship with them is afraid of. Insecurity makes someone feel like they are constantly under competition and need repeated reassurance that their space in your life is secured and not threatened by anyone or thing. Insecurity has also made many to have unnecessary assumptions and chase clouds, thinking that there is something that is existing whereas there is none. In an adult narcissist's life, insecurity is manifested mostly in workplaces or when they want to engage in new relationships. That feeling that they are under competition with someone else is always very high.

Reasons why narcissist upbringing is destructive to children

You may wonder why the impacts of being raised by a narcissistic parent are so enduring and extremely hard to surmount, and it's all because the damage began from their tender years. Many times, kids raised by narcissists need additional emotional stability. What we learn during our formative years, from our family, stays with us into adulthood, says Women's and Children's Health Network;

"The first and most significant learning in a child's life occurs within the family circle. Children learn from the manner individuals treat them and from what they see, hear, and experience beginning as soon as they are born."

The initial five years, particularly, are the most significant. These are the years when children learn proper behavior, how to identify with, place boundaries, and all social skills that live with them for life.

When you are raised by a narcissist, you are susceptible to their behaviors, mood swings, and episodes since you are just a child. It is normal for you to think this as typical and act in response in the way you had experience of, and the impacts of this sort of treatment have manifested into your adulthood in lots of diverse ways.

At the point when you have been raised by narcissists, the impacts are never really going all out until you become a grown-up. Only then do you begin to recognize the repercussions.

A large number of our enthusiastic failures come from being brought up in such an imbalanced way. Here are 13 conspicuous signs that you experience the ill effects of these outcomes;

1. Low confidence: Children of narcissists were always disgraced as children. Due to their parent's unattainable desires, they felt that they were barely adequate. Also, because the parents are narcissists, it is practically difficult to satisfy them. These sentiments of low-esteem carry on to adulthood and make the kid emotionally feeble.

2. Isolation: Because of low confidence, a few children of narcissists become excessively terrified of disappointment that they become even scared of trying. So, all things being equal, they disengage themselves from circumstances and individuals that may make them feel "less." Narcissistic parents are unequipped for giving their children a suspicion that all is well and good, which makes for a kid who simply feels distanced and rejected.

3. Abandonment issues: Narcissists never give their children approval. In any case, when they do, it happens so infrequently that their kids don't have a clue on how to respond. Now and again, kids will clutch this approval so much that they become oppressive. As grown-ups, they have extraordinary abandonment issues and experience difficulty keeping up with or maintaining a healthy relationship with others.

4. *Self-consciousness:* Narcissists bring up their kids with an eagle eye at whatever point suits them. This implies that whenever they do choose to notice their children, they are frequently excessively critical of them. As grown-ups, their children become amazingly reluctant about all that they do – the manner in which they talk, look, and any outward exertion they provide for their general surroundings. They, once in a blue moon, got encouraging words as kids, so they don't have sound self-esteem as grown-ups.

5. *Feeling of inadequacy:* This is another appearance of being made to feel that they are bad enough. Narcissistic parents frequently contrast their children with others. They regularly show this in visual cue subtleties. Kids grow up always being contrasted with other better kids. As grown-ups, they wind up having an irrational feeling of inadequacy.

6. *Depression and uneasiness:* These sentiments of relinquishment and insufficiency can prompt one major thing– depression. Frequently, these qualities estrange and restrict somebody from building and keeping up an important relationship with themselves and other individuals. It tends to be hard to figure out how to cherish oneself. Children of narcissists experience depression and sadness even as kids. What's more, they just escalate as they develop into an adult.

7. Lack of self-confidence: Narcissistic parents frequently silence their children when they attempt to stand up to express their opinion over any issue. As a result of this, their children tend to grow up with the inability to air their views over any issue. It really turns into a dread to speak out. The rationale behind your failure or incapability to speak up is certainly two things; your low level of confidence or your decision to just keep quiet. In any case, this behavior can be brought about by a narcissistic upbringing.

8. Self-destruction: When a narcissist raises a child, such a child's childhood turns into a telenovela and an ill-fated and ruinous environment. Also, in light of the fact that this is their adaptation of normal life at an early age, they generally pull in it into their adulthood. They unknowingly gravitate toward harmful circumstances and acquaintances. In many cases, when they had experienced sound relationships, they start craving for the precariousness of a harmful one that they self-disrupt.

9. Extraordinary affectability: Being raised by a narcissist makes a child excessively touchy to anything that is going on around them. As small kids, this is basic to endurance since they generally need to measure their parent's mind-sets. As grown-ups, they become touchy to other individuals' sentiments. Seeing someone, this winds up hazardous in light of the fact that they are very delicate in any event, for the lightest things. It additionally makes them wildly enthusiastic and effectively controllable by others.

10. *Absence of boundaries:* The most dangerous thing children acquire from their narcissistic parents is the total incapability to set up boundaries. In that incapacity, they can be effectively manhandled and exploited by their employers, associates, significant others. They always attempt to please people, which means they sacrifice such a large amount of themselves just to get approval from others. Indeed, even the least insignificant mistake at work or in relationships makes them really crazy as though it's a big deal. This is the motivation behind why they generally struggle with their professions and their own relationships with others.

11. *Co-dependency in relationships*: According to psychotherapist Ross Rosenburg; *"Co-dependency anorexia often results in the co-dependent parent unjustifiably and improperly trying to meet their emotional, social, and personal needs through their children. This form of enmeshment is often referred to as emotional incest, which is harmful to a child's psychological development."*

Accordingly, the narcissistic kid grows up lacking in confidence and a solid feeling of self-esteem – two things that are significant in their capacity to have a healthy and sound relationship.

When you couple these deficiencies with their co-dependency on their folks while growing up, you'll see it appears in their adult relationships as well.

12. Feeble sense of self: An unyielding sense of self is essential in navigating normal daily life. It prevents us from contrasting ourselves with others. It gives us trust in our capacities. In particular, it shapes a solid identity. Both inundating and overlooking narcissistic parents neglect to assist their kids with building up their own personality. Thus, they don't have the foggiest idea what their identity is and what they need. Some of the time, this may even form into a borderline personality disorder.

13. Over-competitiveness: An overwhelming narcissistic parent's bizarre desire for their children makes them over-competitive. At times, this might be something worth being thankful for. Being competitive is a strong sign of achievement. Notwithstanding, over-competitiveness is something else.

At the point when you are excessively competitive, you determine your self-esteem exclusively from your accomplishments.

As soon as you discover most of these traits are found in your life, then it's about time you find a way to do something about it. The first thing to do is to come to terms with the fact that you have a challenge by acknowledging it. Your childhood may have been troublesome and might have caused a large portion of the negative things in your adult life; however, they only define you to the extent that you allow them to.

It is never simple to attempt to heal from being raised by a narcissist. As a matter of fact, it is one of the most troublesome difficulties to defeat since it is so imbued in you since childhood. You will have to oppose to everything that you've known. You need to fight against your most natural impulses.

Nonetheless, you can get over it. You can decide to not give your past experience a chance to prevent you from a bright future. All you need is the mental fortitude (and it will take a great deal) to truly dive deep in yourself and assess exactly how damaging your childhood has been. Furthermore, when you know the degree of your injury, you can find a way to recover from them.

You are just as strong as you permit yourself to be. Accept that as your reality and believe it from your heart that you are. Self-approval and interfacing with your actual self are key to the mending venture. We will most likely be unable to change the narcissistic parent; however, we can find a way to guarantee that we ourselves are living credible lives and not displaying the parent's ruinous methods for acting and identifying with the world.

Daughters of narcissistic dads

The individuals who have had a narcissistic parent can affirm how harming it tends to be to one's mind. Narcissistic parents lack compassion, show a serious feeling of privilege to micromanage the lives of their youngsters, and may even expose their kids to abandonment, as well as emotional and physical exploitation.

Girls of narcissistic dads face all the normal difficulties of having an unempathetic, remorseless, and abusive parent, however, alongside these, they may likewise experience special triggers and hindrances on the way to their recovering journey. Here are five basic difficulties little girls of narcissistic dads experience and tips on the best way to conquer them on the recovering journey. Male children of narcissistic dads may likewise be able to relate to these.

The pompous self-image and reputation of their dads hardly ever matched the coldness and indifference behind closed doors, habituating their children to come to acknowledge interpersonal danger as the custom. Narcissists, in general, are masters of impression management, and the charismatic narcissistic father is not in any way different.

As the daughter of a narcissist, you can see that your father places his reputation in the community above anything else, even the welfare of the family members. Your dad may be liberal, sociable, and incredibly enchanting to each one of the persons who knew him publicly, yet away from public scrutiny, he was verbally, sincerely, and additionally physically violent to his life partner and kids. This isn't rare in families with a narcissistic parent; their 'false self' is hardly ever a match for the true self within the sphere of the family circle. The victim of most parent rape cases is often committed by narcissist fathers to their daughters. The reason for this behavior is also psychological and a complete mental disorder.

Daughters of narcissistic dads are able to achieve this by completely stopping their daughters from any clubs, associations, social gatherings, and in many cases, they stop their daughters from having friends. They also constantly let their daughters know that they are the only ones capable of loving them and taking care of them. They may live in areas, towns or cities where it is difficult for other people to live in or they may live in less populated towns. The reason for these choices is to further limit their daughter from any interaction with the public. Narcissist fathers like this are termed psychopaths. From a young age, they may introduce sexually related content to their daughters and claim that it is the only way to make a man happy.

Subsequently, little girls of narcissistic dads are probably made quiet in case they have ever tried to take a stand to the maltreatment or speak ill of the dad within the family unit or in public.

Coupled with gender positions and the desires for young ladies to be silent, coy, and cordial, little girls of narcissistic dads may have been molded to adjust to threat instead of shielding or protecting themselves from it. That is the reason perilous circumstances and individuals with a Jekyll and Hyde character – individuals who are hardly reliable in their character or honesty – feel like a strangely natural safe place to little girls of narcissistic dads in adulthood.

What to do?

Confirm and admit the encounters you had with your narcissistic parent and don't allow the views of others to dimish the truth of the maltreatment you experienced. It is basic and very normal for survivors of any type of abuse and maltreatment to disbelief and question themselves about the terrible infraction they experienced. This is particularly evident when their abuser is a loved figure in the society or projects a generous and loving picture of the world.

If the abuse is severely affecting your emotional well-being and prosperity, then think about restraining contact with your narcissistic parent to only holidays and special events. Constrained contact helps you to take your capacity back, as you can control the recurrence with which you associate with the parent and walk away from possibly compromising circumstances before they heighten. However, before embarking on constraining contact with your narcissistic parent, adequate planning is needed to ensure that the narcissist child has finances, shelter, social support, and a second alternative if things don't work out well while distancing themselves from their narcissist parent.

A few survivors find that their specific circumstance demands or means 'No Contact' with their abusive parents; if that is the situation, realize that you don't need to feel regretful or embarrassed. You have every prerogative to protect yourself from hazardous individuals, regardless of whether they share your DNA.

A narcissist daughter can also learn valuable approaches to self-validate. This is done by talking with an advisor or therapist about the maltreatment/abuse they have tolerated and reconnect with its reality. Consult with approving relatives or companions who were likewise receivers of the abuse and don't discontinue it. Respect what you encountered and know that you didn't deserve it in any shape or way.

Be aware of the existence of and consider the possibility to restrict contact with any individuals you presently have in your life who equally demonstrate a bloated ego and a 'false sense of self-worth.' A lot of times when we've been raised by a dad figure this way, we tend to gravitate in the direction of individuals who feed us empty words and fake promises, or who are also emotionally stunted.

Stay true to yourself, respect your individuality. You don't have to mimic others; you can be your own self. Reach within, find the true you. Learn how to express the true you. You don't have to walk the path your narcissistic parent set out for you. So many things have happened in the past, but they don't have to determine your future. There's no point wishing you had a better childhood, all you have now is the opportunity to be a better person so don't throw it away.

On the journey of healing, you need to be in touch with your true self. Although the past cannot be changed, you need to start believing in a better life, and purposing that you will not replicate your parent's destructive ways is a great start.

4

The Life of a Victim of Narcissistic Parenting

W hat happens to a person who had a narcissist parent(s)? As far as the major statics about the child are concerned, including their communication as a teen and the relationship problems that are experienced, one may ask - how does it affect their work-life? How does it affect their love life? The way narcissistic parents bring up their children has a lot of impact on the emotional, psychological, and social life of those children.

According to the American Psychological Association, people between the ages of 18 and 33 are reported to have the highest stress levels. This is a critical time in the life of any individual because it is the period where you chart your course for life and a time when the society expects you to be at your best in terms of energy and vigor available to you. This kind of push is positive if, in a healthy amount, but for children who grow up with narcissistic parents, it is usually to the extreme. The resultant effect of an extreme push is always on the negative side of the line.

These parents tend to feed their egos with the lives of their children without giving careful thought or consideration to what the child really wants. They force their will, ideologies, and desires on the child without paying attention to the child's individuality. In most cases, they subject the child to isolation or abandonment when they perceive they are trying to be their own person.

They fail to understand that a child is a different entity and has a life of their own. The fact that you were the channel through which the child came does not necessarily make them one with you in reasoning and way of life. All they are concerned about is their own self-image and how they can constantly put pressure on their kids to help them polish their own image. A child that grows up in that kind of environment sees the world from the perspective that their parents have presented.

Let's look at some effects narcissistic parents have on their children in their communication, emotional, and working life.

• *Low self-esteem:* Parents with narcissistic tendencies never see the good in their kids because they always expect them to do more. They tend to exert an undue perfectionism, thereby putting an extremely high pressure on these kids. Some of them will push themselves to the extent of using a reward-based system where a child earns love from his or her actions and achievement.

This kind of environment hurts the self-esteem of a child; he gets to feel defeated in his mind even before he sets out on a mission. He constantly hears negative comments at home, and when these things register over time, the child will a precise image of themselves. The child begins to heap blames on himself for everything that happens and even for things yet to happen.

This kind of image usually depicts a lower than usual opinion of oneself. In life, you have got to win the battle in your mind before you get to the battlefield, and if you constantly dwell on the fact that you can only fail, it is very likely to happen. Growing up in a reward-based environment rather than a love-based one tends to foster the development of low self-esteem in a child, and if proper care is not taken, it could affect that child through teenage years down to adulthood.

• **_Communication problems:_** Most of the children that were brought up by narcissistic parents tend to be reserved and withdrawn from people. They are shy and are unable to communicate their feeling effectively. They grew up with the fear of making mistakes at anything they do, even with the words they utter. So, they are usually very careful and cautious about what they say.

Most of the time, they just prefer not to talk for fear of saying something wrong because while growing up, their parents could withhold love from them for speaking up or challenging their opinion in any way. So, they would rather be safe than sorry by just keeping things to themselves. They exhibit shyness instead of confidence. This robs these kids of living the kind of life they really want to live and, if taken to adulthood could even lead to loneliness and consequently depression. They are known to bottle up most of their emotions, which is usually not a good thing for their emotional health.

• *Inability to receive love:* People that grew up with narcissistic parents are accustomed to the feeling of not deserving love unless they have done something to earn it. After spending so much time with parents that make you work to earn their love, you get automatically bound to think you don't deserve to be loved. Most of these kids grow up to be unable to maintain love relationships with people because of the experiences they have had in the past.

There is always a feeling of inadequacy attached to any gift or act of kindness they receive. I heard of a young man who had a narcissistic mom. His mom never saw anything good in him; in fact, he had to do something extraordinary to earn him a good meal. After he left the house to live on his own, of course, he found it difficult to maintain a relationship.

One day, his roommate's mom visited and wanted to make them a special meal, and the first thing he said was that he did not feel he did anything to deserve that kind of special meal. Something as simple as a meal. Huh? You wouldn't blame him because that was how he was brought up, and it will take an effort on his own part to break out of that kind of thinking to enable him to receive love freely and be able to give love to others too.

• ***The constant need of validation from others:*** This is one major effect of being brought up by narcissistic parents. You tend to crave approval from others, which is dangerous. It is dangerous because it makes you live the life that others expect of you instead of living the life of your dreams. You build your self-worth from what people think and say of you, making you a slave of another person's opinion.

It is not wrong to ask for people's opinions, but making it a lifestyle and constantly craving to hear positive comments from people is a problem. Since these children didn't get these validations from their parents while growing up, they are usually hungry to receive them from other people.

• ***Unhealthy competitive tendency:*** Growing up with narcissistic parents is a lot of work as they constantly keep you on your toes. They make you feel there is always something better to be done, someone out there for you to outdo, and the loop goes on. It never has an end with them. They do not celebrate the small victories of their kids; instead, they want them to do more.

Competition is good when it is healthy; when you strive for what you believe in, not primarily because you must outsmart somebody or be ahead of someone. When you have these kinds of parents, you are always on the go, trying to outdo someone, but the irony of it is that you will never live a happy life with that kind of mentality because there is always someone you will need to be ahead of. This makes it difficult for them to live happy lives because nothing is ever enough. When an individual grows into adulthood with this kind of mentality, it will be difficult for him to have good relationships with colleagues at work because he will always see them as his competitors. The narcissistic parenting leaves a bunch of effects on children including the guilt-tripping and emotional blackmail.

As the life of a victim of narcissistic parenting grows worse by the day due to low self-esteem, unhealthy competition, poor communication, and other factors such as the inability to receive love, the narcissist child channels this mindset and the level of negative energy acquired from this lifestyle into their work and in the life of other people, thus spreading the narcissist plague even further.

The unhealthy side for friends and relatives who are close to the narcissist begins when they observe their lifestyle and then decide to distance themselves from the narcissist child. Narcissist children are mere victims of narcissist parents and may not even be narcissists themselves. It is understandable that no one wants to be influenced by the life the narcissist lives or be influenced by their ideology towards work, life, or relationships. However, no narcissist can recover from their mental disorder or behavior without care, love, and support from the people they interact with on a daily basis. The plague of narcissism can only be cured by love and good therapy. It can also be managed clinically by qualified psychologists who have been trained and have studied to help victims of narcissists.

When one has discovered that they are narcissists and that may be the reason why people are distancing themselves away from them in order not to be influenced by their toxic behavior, a solution to this can be to seek clinical help and study on the best ways to overcome narcissist behavior. Allowing the effect narcissistic parents to continue having a grip on you will only reduce your level of self-worth and leave you feeling guilty and not capable of true love and genuine acceptance by the society.

5

Dealing with Narcissistic Parents

O ne of the hardest parts of loving a person is knowing their flaws and loving them despite those flaws. Loving narcissistic parents is not the easiest thing in the world, it is often more than what a person can handle. Whether the narcissist parent has been engulfing or ignoring, it is very difficult for a narcissist child to completely let go of the love they have for their parent. The biological bond existing between the biological parents and their children makes it almost impossible to recognize all the abuse, neglect, and pain they may have caused their child.

Once again, this puts the child in a dilemma of how to keep loving their parents from a distance even if they stop communicating with their parents completely. The child may constantly ignore the feeling to return to their parents or give their parents a second chance in their life because they have been repeatedly disappointed and have resigned to the fact that this is the character or true nature of their parent. In social gatherings, when questions are being asked about their parents, the narcissist child may not answer, or they may answer and claim that they are in constant communication with their parent.

The reason behind the lies is not to get appreciation from the social gathering. The lies about constant communication are told in order to make people believe that everything is okay even when it is not. It may also be because they are ashamed or do not want people to know that they have narcissist parents in order not to feel judged. Narcissist children keep going through this dilemma without knowing how to let go and love their parents for who they are or how to change their parents' behavior towards them.

The first step in loving your narcissistic parents is recognizing that they will never change and therefore asserting boundaries and effectively keeping those boundaries up. When your loved ones disagree with your opinions, there is a high tendency for arguments and hurtful words to be exchanged, more so when dealing with narcissists.

Continuous disagreements will eventually lead to hate. The purpose of realizing and educating yourself on the narcissistic behaviors of your parents is not to despise them but to bring healing to yourself and eventually to them if possible.

You may wonder if it is possible to maintain a healthy relationship or contact with your narcissistic, manipulative parents. Most of us love our parents, even when we struggle to understand them. A healthy relationship takes effort and is difficult but doable. It may be more demanding than what we would like it to be, but it can be rewarding. For one to successfully keep a cordial and loving relationship, one must create and assert boundaries in all aspects of the relationship.

Boundaries are the armor needed to guard your heart while trying to maintain a relationship with your narcissistic parents. One needs to develop and maintain these in order not to lose themselves or be emotionally devastated while managing the relationship with their parents.

Children raised by narcissistic parents often carry some of their parent's behaviors even without realizing it. The most important step to take before effecting boundaries is recognizing those same narcissistic traits you may have picked up. What behaviors do you exhibit that are like those of your parents? Recognize them and work towards getting rid of them in order to start healing. It would be the height of hypocrisy and even a bit narcissistic to expect that your parents desist from their behavior towards you or others when you engage in the same behavior.

For all purposes, I am of the opinion that one should not avoid their parents, but engage more with them, with an open and loving mind. This is to foster love, and your absence will create a chasm that will probably be filled with bitter memories and ill will. In one's dealings with parents, the best approach is to never argue, even when you absolutely disagree with their opinions, instead try to discuss and negotiate. This might be more demanding when dealing with narcissists, but in the long run, it will pay off in the form of a better relationship.

Differences in behavior and ideology, disagreements, and sour memories will hurt, and you may start to judge yourself, doubting whether you are any different and if, in fact, you are the true cause of your parents' behavior. These doubts are inevitable, but you must only embrace them and work with these doubts.

A complete lack of empathy on the part of a narcissist means that their children are deprived of that understanding and feeling that comes from imagining how certain actions and behaviors would affect a person's feelings; it is a completely selfish act for a narcissist. You may wonder how this affect building your boundary and in turn, your relationship with your parents. I think in refusing to be pulled in by their selfishness, wait out their tantrums, and selfish arguments. This is because any argument will blow up into something bigger. Refusing to succumb to selfishness like them will help you avoid a lot of unnecessary arguments with them.

Constantly reminding one's self that the narcissistic behavior of a parent or parents is not the result of one's own behavior as a child, but the problem is the inherent traits of parents and of their mental health.

Recognizing that your parents are human and are equally affected by others and your behavior towards will play a huge role in determining the way you interact with them. Remember, softly spoken words will soften a hard heart and letting go of anger will prevent arguments and ill-feeling. Ask yourself; are your interactions with your parents filled with angry outbursts that leave both parties highly strung, dissatisfied and unhappy or are they loving and calm interactions that help your relationship?

Looking at your parents as enemies that need to be eliminated and dealt with will never be the solution. They are only people with mental health problems. Do not see them as pathetic and vain, rather as persons that need your love and sympathy.

Forgiveness is key in relationship management involving your parents. There is the need to recognize if one of your parents is narcissistic and the other only an enabling parent. Both need to be forgiven, and forgiveness of both parents is as hard as (or harder than) recognizing that you still need to love your parents.

An enabling parent is a parent who is not narcissistic, yet excuses the behavior of their spouse and has failed to protect their child from the negative behavior of their narcissistic spouse. You may feel that such a parent has betrayed you, and forgiveness is beyond your scope, but the healing process requires letting go of all hurt, no matter the source. You may need to forgive even yourself, for times you may have felt weak, for times you may have wrongly judged yourself and for times you may have engaged in narcissistic behavior yourself.

Taking control is a vital part of setting up boundaries. Taking charge includes controlling your emotions towards your parents, your reactions to their behavior as well as the way they interact with you, to the point that you feel comfortable in their presence, and being confident enough to inform them of your dissatisfaction with their behavior towards you the moment you feel uncomfortable.

I have heard various times a narcissistic parent telling a story and the child commenting that they remember it differently. Such parents, more often than not, twist the retelling of a childhood memory, trying to convince the child's actions are the ultimate cause of an occurrence, or that it had not, in fact, happened in the way the child remembered it. This is a manipulative trait of such people. Recognizing this will help your reality not to be warped by someone else.

When you interact with your parents, take mental notes of the way you feel at various times, noting your emotions during angry outbursts, and the best way to quickly heal from the hurt. Detach yourself mentally from occurrences that make you feel less confident.

Create an affirmative mantra. Some people don't know how to walk away from a stressful situation, learning to use an affirmative mantra gives you the opportunity to gain the confidence to either walk away or to take charge of the situation.

Triggers are the things that set off an angry outburst or egotistical behavior. Take notes of these triggers, both yours and your parents', and work on these to ensure you oversee your own emotions. It is almost impossible to control the narcissistic behavior of another, but it is possible to control how it affects your emotions and your reactions to it. Once you master this, you will probably notice that there are fewer instances in which your parents attempt to control your behavior. They may likely never stop in their attempts to manipulate and control you.

Manipulation and emotional control are a huge part of narcissistic behavior, and one must not forget this. Think back on those instances where your parents instigated competition between you, the feelings of inadequacy and hopelessness; those were planned by your parents to manipulate and control you! Try to overcome these manipulative plays.

What happens to a dog that has been beaten, starved of love and nourishment? He will perform all tricks to please his master because he wants to be embraced and shown love, which he does not get. Remember also that manipulation does not involve lack of love and care, it is the "rewards" for good behavior after long bouts of neglect.

Many children with narcissistic parents are troubled by the erratic displays of affection and acceptance. They are burdened by parents who think they are always right and try to enforce their opinions and will on their children. These children will often decide to rather please the parent than try to have their own opinions. One material you cannot do without when building your boundary wall is your individuality. Create and form your own opinions, seek others' perspectives (without seeking approval), and remember that mother (or father) isn't always right.

Gaining independence from a manipulative parent is not merely limited to physically living away from them. It involves liberating yourself from oppressive thoughts and behaviors. Let us take, for example, a child, a minor who cannot legally live on his own. What then should they do to survive in a narcissistic home?

Liberation starts from embracing your own individuality. Shaping and taking hold of things that are uniquely yours, your thoughts, opinions, and even eccentricities. Self-awareness and acceptance play a huge role in asserting boundaries. Once you accept yourself as you are, warts and all, it means ridicule is less likely to negatively affect you. This is not to say that your skin is impermeable; no, you will likely get hurt by words and behavior, but self-acceptance is the medicine that helps to shake it off and move on.

You must learn to recognize these mechanisms of manipulation and making sure not to fall victim to them any longer. The narcissist will try to assert their control by dividing the family, each person playing a different role, in a competition against each other. You may have been the one praised in order to subjugate a sibling or even a parent, forgive yourself, and refuse to be a puppet in the hands of a master puppeteer. Do not blame a sibling who was upheld as the standard of a perfect child, it was not his or her fault, nor was it yours if you were made out to be the "inferior" child.

It can be overwhelming being in constant communication with narcissistic parents, and one of the processes of building boundaries is to limit time with such parents. Yes, limit time! It is advisable not to pull away from them entirely but keep a healthy distance from their toxic behavior. A phone call during Christmas turns into a session of fault finding and ridicule? Cut short the tirade by wishing them a merry Christmas and bidding them farewell. Do not feel like you need to listen, this will only delay your healing process, avoid it at all costs.

Sometimes seeking a new role model is what shapes a better life for us. Many of us grew up looking up to our parents as role models, and when it seems like those models aren't ideal, it leaves us floundering, confused about whether there is actually something wrong with our parents or if the fault could be ours for not fitting in the standards. When you have concluded that your parents are narcissists, it is more than acceptable to look elsewhere for "normality". Look at others around you, appreciating them and gain confidence by the fact that they believe you are more than good enough.

Patience is vital in dealing with narcissistic parents. Often, we feel like bursting out in anger or even sadness when confronted with their emotional abuse. It is best not to give in to these feelings, but to patiently and calmly work towards a reply that shows your strength of character, while also releasing the tension of a situation. Remember, you may not always be successful, but over time the victories will be more than the defeats.

There will be setbacks, overwhelming feelings of inadequacy; it takes time to build confidence and heal, do not feel like you must make all the progress in one day. A better relationship with your parents will also take time. Accord them some respect as your parents, and if that is slow in building up, patiently persist, and it will come in time.

Beware not to seek validation from your parents, as validation opens a gateway to manipulation. Celebrate your victories the way you want, don't ask if it will be enough to garner the love of your parents, love they never gave, will never come because of personal progress you have made. There should be love between family, not to be determined by performance or lack thereof.

In the case of your narcissistic parents, love them despite their behavior. Do not, however, give credence to the love they "award" you for good performance. Make a conscious effort not to fall victim to this manipulative form of conditional love; love should be given regardless of what one has achieved. Enjoy the love given unconditionally, do not seek more, you will only fall into a controlling trap.

I remember the story told by The Soviet novelist Chinggis Automaton in one of his articles. In 1935, Stalin invited his advisors to a meeting. He called for a live chicken, he then worked at plucking out the chicken's feathers one by one. He did this until the chicken was completely without feathers, not minding that the chicken squawked and convulsed in agony the entire time. Once he was done, he then held out a handful of grains to the chicken, the chicken to the amazement of the audience, went back to Stalin, and started eating right out of the hand that had only just tortured it.

Stalin then said to his audience, "People are like this chicken. It doesn't matter how much pain you inflict on them. The moment you offer them what they need, they will still follow you and turn to you for their survival".

Why am I telling this gruesome story? Survival. If you believe that a person is your source of survival, then you will endure anything they put you through, and keep going back to them because you need them and what they give you to keep you alive!

Narcissistic parents will often manipulate their children, making them actively seek validation and acceptance, making them feel like their entire existence hinges on those words of praise and love their parents give. So even when the ridicule and emotional twists and turns come, they still turn to their parents for comfort.

A narcissist will often want to create the impression of a perfect family. Ensuring that you recognize and refuse to play along with this pretense gives you a measure of control over the relationship. An effort not to exert yourself in preserving a perfect family image gives you a greater sense of peace. Peace of mind translates to a measure of control over your emotions and helps your healing process. There can be little to no success in asserting boundaries if there is no healing.

The act allegedly carried out by Stalin, though it involved physical torture, it was in its basic form – emotional manipulation. Victims often fail to see the manipulative agenda behind words of praise after heavy ridicule. It is only conditioning for you to seek validation and acceptance.

In the quest to find a balance between love, acceptance given freely, and a narcissistic parent, it is best to remember that control is always the best weighing scale. Have a measure of control over how much you crave that acceptance, how badly it matters to you and how much of your peace of mind you are willing to forego to get it. Remember also that your parents know how much their acceptance means to you and will work to take advantage of it for their selfish interest. A desire to break out of a manipulative narcissistic relationship means keeping a healthy balance between love given freely by narcissistic parents and your own need for love from them.

This leads me to sound a much-needed warning on one of the challenges of maintaining a relationship with your parents. You have come so far in recognizing that such a parent or parents have a mental health problem, or more accurately, a personality disorder, and this is no fault of theirs. That hate is not the best solution, nor is cutting them off your life.

This scenario comes up more often than I like to admit. A child seeking to patch things up and heal the relationship with their parent, while the parent is using it as a way to avenge for wrongs that they perceive that child did against his person or as a mechanism to further draw the child in their manipulative web.

It is prudent to handle matters with a narcissistic parent with caution. Do not give in to demands to make amends for past sins in order to get into their good graces. Set your limits and let the entire relationship be managed according to your comfort level. Remember, you do not depend on their validation for survival.

To deal with narcissist parents is easier written than acted upon. Narcissist parents need love, care, and attention. A narcissist child should always remember that if they are not ready to deal with the narcissist mental disorder that their parents are suffering, they are already on the path of becoming narcissists themselves.

However, before you can deal with a narcissist parent, you have to heal the influence of narcissism already present in you; open your heart and open your mind to love irrespective of their flaws. As an Asian proverb says "only cracked pots water the best flowers."

6

Healing from Narcissistic Parenting

S o often we talk about healing from a bad situation we have been in, yet we are unsure about how we should go about it. Healing involves quiet introspection. Often, this is not easy to do, as we often find that our thoughts can be our biggest enemy. A sick person or an invalid that seeks healing relies on a lot of processes such as care, love, attention, medical treatment, and any other means of recovery. The only thing their family and friends desire for him is to recover. Colleagues at work will insist for them to recover first before they resume their duties and colleagues at school will encourage one to recover before resumption. This means that the health and mental state of a person is important before anything else. Thus, without recovery, there is no progress.

Therefore, the first step to recovery is to check what you can do when confronted with the reality that you may have been negatively affected by narcissistic, manipulative parenting. How do you even recognize the symptoms?

The first tell-tale sign of unhealthy symptoms of narcissistic parenting manifests in the form of guilt. A narcissist victim feels a pang of complete guilt because they have, in some way failed their parents. You always feel guilty because your parents may have done so much for you, yet you have failed them again and again. This leaves you with feelings of indebtedness, the constant desire to make amends and sacrifice as much as they have sacrificed for you. This is a classic controlling behavior by narcissists.

They make you feel so guilty that you hand over all the control to them and are in complete obedience to their will. Although it is important to appreciate the efforts and the love that your parents have shown towards you, one should realize that it is not possible to appreciate them completely. It is a debt you may have to pay gradually as long as they are alive.

Maybe sometimes you have also had countless memories of feeling truly special or loved only when you have done what your parents wanted? They made you feel as though you had to show how much you loved them, and in turn, they showered you with much-needed affection. Many kids who grow up in narcissistic homes believe this is normal. They must be good, so mommy loves them, daddy loved them because they always did what daddy wanted.

It is often difficult to recognize that your childhood was anything but abusive. Narcissistic parents are great at presenting a perfect and united front, therefore the possibility of a child to realize that conditional love is not normal is faint and in those instances where you do feel like something is not quite right, your parents convince that everything is perfectly normal and you should be grateful for "belonging" "belonging" and being loved by them.

The love of a narcissistic parent can manifest in the controlling form of co-dependency. Did your parents explain to you over and over how life would be impossible without you? Did your decision to leave become a personal attack against them and their wellbeing? They may have convinced you that your individuality is abhorrent and rebellious, and the only way to show love was to stay and take care of their needs.

There is nothing more destabilizing than realizing that that time you won the school talent show, and your mom simply had to tell the story of when she won the state beauty pageant was, in fact, competitive behavior of a narcissist. Your upbringing has often been a competition between you and your parents, with them repeatedly bringing you down by outdoing you in every way. If you often feel inadequate, or that you can never measure up to the great deeds of your parents, then narcissistic parenting may be to blame.

If you often feel like the credit of your achievements belongs to your parents, then narcissistic parenting may be a culprit. For every achievement, your parents would constantly tie the victory back to themselves and you cower from compliments and attribute your success to your parents.

For those rebellious moments you decided not to share the spotlight with your parents, they showed their displeasure by punishing or getting even with you for your "transgressions" against them. A child of a narcissist often hates conflict and strives not to get on the wrong side of their parents. Your lack of courage and a strong dislike for heated discussions are classic symptoms of a narcissistic upbringing. They withheld affection or praise when they felt slighted by you. This constant need to get even may seem puerile but is, in fact, a trait of a narcissist.

The only time you ever feel worthy or special to your parents was when you relinquished control to them. Nothing you do is ever good enough unless it was dictated and sanctioned by your parents. Coloring your hair a different color than the choice of your parents is such a big deal. Control of even the thing that may seem insignificant to you is what makes a narcissist tick. You often hand over every aspect of your life to the control of your parents.

You find that you are often unable to say no and being unable to set up and maintain boundaries. Narcissistic childhoods are not characterized by boundaries because your parents always went through your belongings and even searched your room and maybe they probably still do, you are unable to enforce personal boundaries with them and with others.

This often results in feeling depressed and anxious. You dislike people stepping over you, yet you are unable to stand up for yourself or to assert boundaries. Feelings of self-loathing quickly fall in, all drowning you in emotions you are not equipped to handle. It is a vicious cycle of people-pleasing and then shame for your perceived inadequacies.

Feeling extremely insecure about your flaws and having a constant fear of people realizing your flaws and thus loving you a lot less is one of the consequences of narcissistic parenting. Ridicule, insults, and humiliations were a usual part of your childhood. As an adult, you realize that even the most constructive criticism makes you retreat and hide into your shell, feeling damaged.

Your relationship with your siblings could also be an indicator of a narcissistic upbringing. You are in competition with your sibling(s), one being the "golden" child and the other the "scapegoat". Depending on which child you were, you may harbor feelings of ill will towards your sibling (if you were the scapegoat). Sometimes the roles may switch, and as such, there are constant fluctuations in the dynamics of your sibling relationship.

Don't get me wrong, sibling rivalry is not unusual, nor often unhealthy, but it can be when parents have enforced the roles of good and bad on the children, depending on how best they obey and sacrifice for their parents.

You may notice constant feelings of self-doubt as a result of gaslighting. In case you were wondering what gaslighting is, have you ever questioned your sanity because of the contrary and confusing narration of a fond memory by your parents? They tell you this or that did not happen the way you remember it, leaving you to feel insane because you remember it the exact opposite way. You are left to wonder if you are crazy for having vivid but (by your parent's account) incorrect memories. Yashar Ali has this to say about gaslighting "... is a term, often used by mental health professionals (I am not one), to describe manipulative behavior used to confuse people into thinking their reactions are so far off base that they are crazy."

You are constantly questioning your reality and sanity, feeling crazy but afraid to voice it out, you are probably reeling from the aftershocks of narcissistic parenting. Don't question your sanity, no, you are not the one suffering from mental illness. However, there are things you can do to help fight the unhealthy effects of a narcissistic childhood.

There is a ray of hope, a way of getting rid of the shame, guilt, self-doubt, and even self-loathing you may have. But the first step is realizing that you owe no one anything but a simple cup of love and kindness. You do not owe your parents your achievements, academic qualification, marrying the right person, having a good house or being the best in your workplace. All you owe them is love and kindness. If you love them, you can forgive yourself and forgive them as well. If you are kind to them, you will show them kindness because they have low self-esteem and therefore want to use their children to build their self-esteem. This means that there is no reason to challenge their authority. A little distance and respect will make it possible for them to recognize that you don't deserve to be treated the way they do. And just as Celine Dion sings in her music "a little bit of love of love is all it takes, a little bit of love goes a long long way".

Seeking the help of a therapist

After filling your self with love, the next is to conquer your fears. This can be done with the help of a professional therapist. You may have realized that you grew up in the manipulative environment of a narcissist. There is peace and tranquility after the storm. You have recognized the unhealthy symptoms and habits you may have developed from this twisted upbringing, the very first step towards healing is recognizing and deciphering the problem.

The next thing to do is to talk to a professional. You may be confused as to why you should be the one needing to see a therapist. Why not my parents? They are the ones with issues. Well, the truth is, you may know that they need professional help, but if they do not come to the realization themselves, there's no way you can help them.

The children of narcissists are the ones who suffer. A therapist will walk you through the healing process and will help you when you struggle with the chaotic and emotionally disturbing memories. They help to sort out your scrambled emotions and figure out exactly how your parents' behavior was manipulative and that it was no fault of yours.

They may even be able to work with you and your parents, so your parents can realize that their behavior is toxic and has negatively affected you. The therapist would work towards building a better relationship with you. Even if this does not happen, do not feel let down but focus on healing yourself.

Booking an appointment to see a therapist is the first step in your journey to self-healing. However, showing up for the appointment is the real process of healing. Why is this such a big deal? It is a giant leap because taking up the courage to get out of your insecure shell and opening up to a stranger about the dysfunctionalities of your childhood is an act of courage contrary to what has been taught you by your controlling parents.

Do you know you may have been taught to bottle up your feelings inside until you implode? Do you know you may have been taught to blame yourself for the problems of the universe? The fact is growing up with narcissistic parents is traumatic, and talking to a therapist breaks the first chains of your parents' manipulative hold on you. You shatter and expose their illusions of perfection, so you can heal!

A therapist is meant to help you become a better version of yourself. He or she is trained not to judge but to focus on the problem at hand and work with you to become stronger. They have worked with so many people just like you who, once thought they had come to the end of the road and have been helped them, regain their zeal and passion in life. These therapists know what it feels like to live with manipulative parents, and they are trained to help you see yourself as the star you were meant to be.

This is not the time to be deceiving and concealing, you would only hinder your healing. Be as truthful as possible, and let out all your pain. That is how to get the healing you need. Don't go on with life as the victim of narcissistic abuse, look forward to your sessions with the therapy and understand you are setting yourself free from all the pain that has held you back all your life.

Always remember that a professional therapist has a confidentiality agreement not to disclose your story to the world without your permission, and they will do their best to help you through the recovery process and also advise you on all you need to know about narcissism and how to deal with it. A professional therapist can also link you with people who have gone through similar situations for moral support and advice. Sometimes, it is easier for a narcissist child to start new friendships with people who have been through the same ordeal. It creates a form of belonging to a family which has shared common pain and this helps make the recovery faster.

Cognitive Behavioral Coaching

One other thing you need to understand is that you may need to work with a behavior coach – a technique called Cognitive Behavioral Coaching (CBC). This originates from counseling with a powerful coaching model that draws on evidence-based psychological models. The fact is that negative words spoken to you by your parents lead to negative thoughts, which also leads to negative emotions. Now, these emotions over the years, lead to negative behaviors, all of which have an effect on you. You may not realize this until a few weeks into your therapy sessions, but I can assure you, you will see the difference. You'll notice that you manage stress, lack of confidence, and communication so much better than you used to. Cognitive-behavioral coaching would help you gain the right perspective towards life and how your response in each situation determines the outcome.

Cognitive Behavioral Coaching aims at developing a better way of thinking and how to adopt more productive behaviors that would help you achieve your desired goal in life. A cognitive-behavioral coach helps you become the person you want to be by helping you build healthier habits and a positive mindset. Let me tell you something profound; if someone can talk to you and make you feel ineffective, rejected, or miserable then you can be talked out of those feelings. This is what a cognitive-behavioral coach does. He or she establishes the fact that nobody's opinion about you matters but what you believe of yourself.

I believe everything you need to be successful can be attributed to your behavioral patterns, whether emotional or practical. A cognitive-behavioral coach is trained to identify patterns in your thoughts, feelings, and behaviors that are self-defeating and work with you to turn your life around – and this is no magic. You have got to be willing. Don't expect to waltz in with the "well, I'm here aren't I" attitude and think you wouldn't be right where you began. Living with Narcissistic parents means you have a skewed outlook on life, it means you could even end up being one yourself. Do you really want that?

Working with a cognitive-behavioral coach can help you understand yourself better. Your cognitive-behavioral coach (or

Life coach) observes you closely and studies how you react and respond to stress, disappointment, anger, and frustration. You are then taught how to respond to each situation positively.

Emotional Intelligence

Narcissistic parents don't have the ability to empathize; hence have no emotional intelligence. Emotional Intelligence is being aware of your emotions and the emotions of others with the ability to manage relationships thoughtfully and empathetically. Narcissistic parents could have little care of your feelings. They burst into unexplainable rage at the slightest provocation, an attempt targeted at eliminating dialogue.

The fact is that parents need emotional intelligence. Emotional intelligence is needed to raise children in a nurturing and constructive manner. Studies have found that yelling at children excessively can do so much harm than spanking would ever do. Constant name-calling and swearing at your child hurts deeper than a slap on the wrist. Every parent needs to understand the importance of emotional health and plant the right idea in the mind of their children. Many children grow up with the feeling of emptiness because their parents have called them worthless for their entire life. In most cases, they turn out well – so it seems – but the impact of those words haunt them for the rest of their lives.

If you grew up with foul-mouthed narcissistic parents, it is almost impossible to measure the amount of hurt you must have been subjected to. I want you to understand that everything they said about you is a lie! You are a beautiful and wonderful soul! Many times, parents pour out their frustrations in life on their children. They delude themselves with the illusions that if the child wasn't born, they would have had it well in life. Some go on to tell the child directly that they are the cause of all their misfortune. The fact is, that's a lie! You are not responsible for anyone's misfortunes. Everyone is responsible for what goes on in their life, and that is why you picked up this book!

Emotional intelligence helps you treat others better than you've been treated. If you were raised by Narcissistic parents, you were raised in a hostile environment and most likely flawed in communication. Emotional intelligence begins with the awareness of your expressions and their impact on you and those around you. First, you recognize that your expressions have an effect on your outlook on life and on those around you. Next, you develop empathy with the understanding that everyone reacts to events differently. You also learn to be considerate of the feelings of others.

Empathy does not mean agreeing with a person's perspective. It means that everyone is entitled to their own opinion. Emotional intelligence also helps you encourage others and show appreciation to others. As much as nobody enjoys negative feedback, emotional intelligence helps you receive and give criticism constructively without hurting the feelings of others. Emotional intelligence helps you become a better person, ultimately, improving your social skills. Here are a few ways you can improve your emotional intelligence;

• *Manage negative emotions better:* You are bound to be upset about one thing or the other at some point in your life, but managing your emotions helps you avoid getting overwhelmed. Even when you get that feeling that someone is really going the extra mile to upset you, try not to get riled up too easily.

• *Mind your vocabulary:* Communication is vital in all spheres of life. Learning to communicate effectively and picking your words carefully help you convey clear messages.

• *Respond and not react:* A lot of people flare up at the slightest accusation. Learn to respond and not react to any comment about you. If you are accused of doing something you didn't do, you may respond as clearly as "I did no such thing" or "I had nothing to do with it." Emotional intelligent people don't respond basing on impulse, because acting like that may lead to even bigger problems. The aim of any conflict is resolution. Understand that clear communication is vital in resolving any conflicts.

• *Maintain a positive attitude:* Do not play down the importance of maintaining a positive attitude. People are naturally attracted to those who seem cheerful. Emotional intelligent people understand that they are in control of their aura and demeanor, and they put energy into looking lively and maintaining a positive attitude all the time.

• **Be aware of your stressors:** Get to know those things that stress you out and learn to avoid them as much as possible. Emotional intelligence is understanding your weaknesses and taking advantage of your strengths.

Conclusion

You have just one life to live. I am sure you don't want to live your whole life in self-pity and regret even though you have been scarred by narcissistic parenting. You picked up this book because you needed a guide to help you in your journey of becoming a better you, and I'm glad to tell you you've made it. Congratulations! You took the bold step in recognizing that you needed to break free from the mental shackles of being raised in horror and fear of narcissistic parenting, and you've made it!

Understanding that you are not the problem is vital on this journey of healing and recovery. You refused to live as the victim by reading this book, and I can boldly say you have achieved that. You have placed your destiny in your own hands and paved the way for a stronger, happier, and healthier you.

Narcissists may never change, and it is of no use trying to convince a narcissistic to see things your way. We have learned that narcissists have a very inflated view of themselves and can never see where they go wrong. You would only end up frustrated if you try to convince a narcissist to be a little considerate about your feelings.

Although they are your parents, you need to stay away from narcissists as much as possible. They lack empathy and must certainly twist matters their own way. They prey on their victims and never stop, no matter how hurt you appear to have been by their actions. Realizing your parents are narcissists should not affect the love and respect you have for them; rather, it should help you avoid situations that would hurt you.

Boundaries are important in any relationship, and it is important to set boundaries when dealing with your narcissistic parents. Narcissistic parents constantly disregard boundaries and believe they have the right to treat their children the way they please. Do not be put in a situation where you would constantly be blamed for every problem in the family. Relating to narcissistic parents has to be on your own terms if you don't want to lose your mind. Set and enforce effective boundaries and they have no choice but to respect them.

Although you have been systematically taught to ignore your feelings by your narcissistic parents, this book has shared several ways to get in touch with your true self. Your feelings will always be a threat to narcissistic parents because they want to force their will and opinions on you. In a narcissistic family, once the parents feel a certain way about a thing, no other person has the right to feel otherwise. If you do, you would be subjected to shame, ridicule, rage, and who knows what.

Healing and reconnecting to your true self takes time. You would discover a new taste in music, food, fashion, movies, etc. You would express that beautiful soul that has been trapped all this time while in the claws of narcissistic upbringing. Your feelings are and will always be important to you, and you will experience imbalance when you are forced to act against them.

It is also very important that you don't cause yourself any more pain than you have already been through. Life has already been so hard on you, don't punish yourself anymore. You may not have had a great start, but you have been able to wipe the dust from your feet and to face life with expectations. These experiences have made you more aware of the emotions of others, and you have learned how to be a great communicator in the process. Keep your past in the past. Don't recall the hurtful words and pain you went through.

Realizing your parents were narcissists does not mean they were entirely bad. In most cases, narcissist parents were also brought up by your narcissist grandparents, so your attitude may seem rebellious. They may have been taught to do what they were told and never to think for themselves, but you have come to realize the importance of your individuality.

Treat them also as the victim of Narcissistic abuse. This means that although they may be unwilling or incapable of change, you know that is better not to hate them for all you have been through. This understanding comes by a certain level of perception – looking beyond your hurts and pains, at the fact that the world was probably a little different back then as well as the fact that little or no study was conducted on this matter.

Life is what we make of it. We don't all get a great start, but we have the power to shape our lives – just as you have done by picking up this book. Remember to be mild on yourself; what you've been through was no easy feat, and you shouldn't shut yourself out of your emotions. Those days are now over, and now you have been equipped with the knowledge on how to relate with narcissists.

On this journey of your healing and recovery, there may be flashbacks of the days when you felt like giving up, days you felt so unworthy of living. I understand how you may have been broken in several unrecognizable pieces, but I believe you've found yourself again. I believe you are better than anyone who has had it easy. I believe people like you make our world a better place as they encourage free-flowing communication, happiness and the recognition of sound mental health.

Final words

Not everyone understands the reason for their behavior. While a few acknowledge that something isn't right, and they need some help, others live their entire life without experiencing love, happiness, and peace. You picked up this book because you want to be different – you want to have an exciting life, and you understand that it's your responsibility to do what it takes to be happy.

Narcissistic upbringing is an indescribable horror, but you are a survivor, you are meant to thrive. You have been through it all and have decided to step into the driver's seat on this journey of life. I want to encourage you to focus on your future. The past is only there to remind you of how strong you are and anytime you reflect on that, don't get too emotional. Remember that you can no longer be controlled by the thoughts and intentions of others.

If you decide to have children, you're surely more prepared than your parents and you know how not to hurt them the way you have been hurt. You understand that individuality means accepting each child's strengths and weaknesses without trying to force them to live up to your high standards. You understand the need for positive reinforcement and expressing your frustrations clearly without going on a foul mouth tirade.

Communication is the bedrock of any relationship. Be it spousal, work-related, or when relating with your children, being able to communicate your ideas clearly and convincingly with an open mind is what I like to call being civil. Be honest with yourself. Ask yourself this question, do I have a problem communicating my thoughts without getting visibly upset or physically abusive? If your honest answer to that question is no, I'll suggest that you seek help. Work with a behavioral coach, and you will experience a tremendous change.

Remember that one of the major identifications of a narcissist is the inability to look beyond self. Have an open mind, and don't shy away from open-minded discussions. Even when presented with a view clearly contrary to yours, don't be so quick to dismiss it. Try to listen to the opinions of others without being too quick to counter it with a dismissing point.

Finally, I need you to believe in yourself. This is something many take for granted, but believing in yourself determines how far you can go in anything you do. Believe you are a good person. Believe you are making the right steps towards healing. Believe that you are not what anyone thinks of you. Believe you are no longer a reflection of your past. Believe you are now the artist of your destiny, and you are a masterpiece!

With love,
Lorna Mayers

Printed in Great Britain
by Amazon